C000246608

# WOODBRIDGE
## A PERSONAL HISTORY

Robert Simper on the barge *Melissa* after
leaving the Tide Mill Quay, Woodbridge.

# WOODBRIDGE

## *A Personal History*

## ROBERT SIMPER

THREE CROWNS PRESS

© Robert Simper 2018

All Rights Reserved. Except as permitted under current legislation
no part of this work may be photocopied, stored in a retrieval system,
published, performed in public, adapted, broadcast,
transmitted, recorded or reproduced in any form or by any means,
without the prior permission of the copyright owner

The right of Robert Simper to be identified as
the author of this work has been asserted in accordance with
sections 77 and 78 of the Copyright, Designs and Patents Act 1998

First published 2018

ISBN 9781916470507

The Three Crowns Press is an imprint of Boydell & Brewer Ltd
PO Box 9, Woodbridge, Suffolk IP12 3DF, UK
and of Boydell & Brewer Inc.
668 Mt Hope Avenue, Rochester, NY 14620–2731, USA
website: www.boydellandbrewer.com

A CIP catalogue record for this book is available
from the British Library

The publisher has no responsibility for the continued existence or accuracy of
URLs for external or third-party internet websites referred to in this book, and
does not guarantee that any content on such websites is, or will remain, accurate
or appropriate

Book designed by Simon Loxley
This publication is printed on acid-free paper

# Contents

# *Introduction*

When Woodbridge was a garrison town many fashionable houses were built for army officers and many old Tudor houses were remodelled with Georgian fronts. These houses always attracted moneyed people to come and settle and the town became an early yachting centre. It came as no surprise to anyone in the town when in 2017 the *Sunday Times* named Woodbridge as being the best place to live in Eastern England. Property prices in the area had already reflected this opinion for at least three previous decades. The town had done an amazing turnaround in its fortunes because eighty years before, back in the dark days of the 1930s slump, local people were trying to find ways to stimulate employment and lessen the poverty in the town.

Woodbridge's past has contained many ups and downs, more downs than ups. This book has much the same history. In 1967 I was asked to write a history of the town for the newly opened Deben Bookshop. That could have been straightforward, but I wanted to try and explain how events and people in the area had created its character. I was reaching high and I did my best.

When the book was finished I took it to the Deben Bookshop and was never certain whether they even read it as they seemed to have lost interest in publishing. The manuscript sat in a chest of drawers in my bedroom for four years until Ken Spence, Editor of the wonderful *East Anglian Magazine*, asked me if I had a book that he could publish. The book was published as *Woodbridge & Beyond* and went on selling for many years with several reprints.

By 1994 the book was out of print but Lucy Bater of Deben Bookshop told me that so many people were asking for copies that it should be reprinted. In response to this, my own imprint Creekside Publishing produced an unchanged edition. In 2001 the bookshop's name was changed to Browsers and later the owner, Martin Whittaker, decided that he wanted to republish an updated version with a more imaginative layout.

Help on the rewrite has come from Peter Nichols of Shottisham with family memories of the past on the coprolite diggings. For the original book I just walked along the Woodbridge riverside talking to Bert Robertson, Claude Whisstock, Frank Knights and the Everson brothers and it was their story that I told.

For this new edition Martin Wenyon told me about the last days of the Whisstock yard and Catherine Larner brought me up to date on the Deben Rowing Club. Chris Moore willingly provided extra local history.

With thanks to Claudia Myatt for editing assistance and for providing some of the illustrations. I took most of the modern photographs and thanks go to my wife Pearl, without whose support I could not have completed this rewrite.

*R.S.*

*Ramsholt, 2017.*

The author and publishers are grateful to all the institutions and individuals listed for permission to reproduce the materials in which they hold copyright. Every effort has been made to trace the copyright holders; apologies are offered for any omission, and the publishers will be pleased to add any necessary acknowledgement in subsequent editions.

# What's in a Name?

The first thing people usually ask about Woodbridge is 'where is the wooden bridge?' When they discover there is no bridge, the next question is 'where was the bridge?'

I first looked into this back in 1964 when I was asked to write a history of the town and area. I started enquiring and was told that most of the historical information on Woodbridge was probably in the Seckford Library, in the Town House up on Market Hill. There, I was welcomed in by an elderly lady called Miss Redstone, the last remaining daughter of Vincent Redstone, a master at the Woodbridge School who had devoted much of his life researching the forgotten history of Woodbridge.

The Seckford Library actually consisted of a collection of books on shelves in Miss Redstone's Best Room that she was loyally safeguarding in her father's memory. We settled down on a comfortable, if slightly worn, sofa and began going through the material. Then Miss Redstone reappeared and politely asked, 'with your cup of tea, what sort of cake would you like?' In no other reference library have I ever been asked this question, but I do think it would be a great improvement to many of them.

Redstone had clearly, like many others, been fascinated by the origin of the name Wood Bridge and had spent a great deal of time trying to get to the bottom of it. He had traced it back to 'Udebryge' in 1086 and 'Wodebregge' in 1256. It seems the early medieval people were referring to some kind of bridge near the Market Hill.

Redstone believed that the first Anglo-Saxon settlement in the area was around Kyson Point so there would have been a track from

Woodbridge from the Sutton shore.

there to the settlement around the Market Hill. This probably came down Drybridge Hill and then along Seckford Street – a route that went on being the main approach to the town for centuries.

There might have been a wooden bridge over the brook at the bottom of Drybridge Hill but, although there is Bridgewood Road nearby there is no sign of a bridge or a stream at the bottom of the hill.

Could there have been a bridge on the other approach to Market Hill? This is possible because there is a stream, now piped under Brook Street, from that direction. The stream must have run through Ship Meadow. Ship is the Suffolk word for sheep and no doubt sheep happily grazed this meadow before the butcher needed them. Now it is all houses.

More recent attempts to pinpoint the name's origin have included the highly imaginative explanation that it comes from 'Woden's

Burgh'. This is because of the pagan burial site up on the other side of the river. However, the Sutton Hoo ship burial is about four hundred years before the Wodebregge of 1256 and the medieval church would have stamped out any reference to the old Anglo-Saxon gods long before that.

Then people look at the River Deben. The word bridge was sometimes used just to mean a crossing place, ferry or ford. But Wilford was more practical, Melton was the main centre of the area, and so far no one has found any suggestion of a bridge or ford across the Deben. Besides, as Redstone pointed out, 'Woodbridge' referred to the market hill settlement, which is unlikely to have got its name from a river crossing. Perhaps the most likely alternative explanation is that the name might have come from a wooden unloading jetty.

Names did jump about all over the place, but Woodbridge first grew up as a market-place rather than a port. It was not until around 1500 that the town began to fulfil its potential as a maritime centre.

The origins of the name are lost in the mists of time, but Woodbridge crops up in other places. There is a hamlet near Shaftesbury in Dorset and another near Guildford. There is a Woodbridge in New Jersey USA (although this is believed to have derived its name from a Dr Woodbridge). There is a Woodbridge outside Toronto in Canada – I found this when I got lost driving and it was nothing like our Woodbridge. The other Woodbridge is in southern Tasmania and I drove miles to find this large village with a pier over a river. It has similarities with the Suffolk Woodbridge – there was even another Orford not too far away.

# TWO

# A Country Town

The approaches to Woodbridge by land do not do it justice. The best way to see Woodbridge for the first time is to come up the River Deben. The tidal Deben winds its way inland about ten miles from the sea and, suddenly, round the bend off Haddon Hall, the town spreads out on the hillside before you.

The first thing that catches the eye is the white Tide Mill and its former warehouse. From this, the houses rise on the hillside and, in the distance, the white sails of Buttrum's tower windmill can just be seen. The slopes appear to be covered with a pattern of red roofs and, here and there, green trees pushing through. The flint tower of St Mary's Church stands out.

Woodbridge is a typical English country town in many ways, but the mixture of the river, shops and residential houses gives it a special character of its own. One of the features of this town on a hillside is the network of quiet alleys which seem to lead nowhere, with period houses hidden away. The narrow streets may bring traffic problems, but this Suffolk town has its own unassuming style.

How did the Woodbridge in Suffolk begin? What made people want to settle in this particular spot?

People have lived in organised societies in the Deben valley for a very long time. It was well populated by the Trinovante tribe when the Romans came. The Romano-British settlements were farms along the valley on the high ground and there was a fort at Walton (now under the sea) guarding the river entrance from raids by Saxon pirates. When the Roman soldiers left for the European mainland, Germanic people came over and mixed with the local population.

The Sutton Hoo site from above. Photograph: Cliff Hoppitt.

Kyson Point and the Fynn Valley seem to have been favourite places for the Anglo-Saxon settlers. Further up the Deben, one band of settlers established a base at Rendlesham and, presumably by force of arms, established the Kingdom of East Anglia – basically Suffolk, Norfolk and part of Cambridgeshire. This was the Wuffing dynasty and it is presumed that they had their royal burial field on the high ground at Sutton Hoo overlooking the River Deben because their burial mounds could be seen and admired on the skyline.

It was always rumoured in the area that ships were buried at Sutton Hoo; indeed most of the seventeen mounds had evidence of robber trenches. Mrs Edith Pretty lived in Sutton Hoo House and one morning one of her guests came down to breakfast and said she had had a dream in which a warrior stood on the ancient burial mounds that could be seen from the window. Mrs Pretty asked Basil Brown, a local man with knowledge of the soil, to do some digging.

In 1939 Basil Brown started digging a trench at one end of the largest mound, and almost at once found traces of a buried longship.

As the shape of the boat appeared in the soil, it was clear that the burial chamber in the middle was surprisingly untouched. For some reason, the sandy soil at the end of Mound One had blown away, so the robbers had dug where they assumed the centre was and had just missed the burial chamber. They had left untouched one of the most important discoveries in British archaeological history and this was unearthed within a few weeks of the outbreak of World War II. It was the first tangible evidence of the very beginning of the English nation.

In the following weeks the burial chamber was excavated by some of the leading archaeologists of the day. The finds included gold and silver goods, a sword and a shield, and all the things that a king might take with him on his journey to the afterlife. For a long time the lack of a body was a mystery, but it was later realised that the ship buried in the mound had acted like a tank, holding water, and the acidic soil had created a mixture that had dissolved the body. Much later, traces of the body were found on some of the goods near the centre of the chamber.

The pagan Anglo-Saxons didn't have a written language, but a long study of the grave goods revealed that the burial had taken place in about 625, just at the time when East Anglia's richest and most powerful king had died. This was Raedwald who, by his victories in battle, had become the leading English king, known later as the Bretwalda. Raedwald had been a pagan but, in order to get the support of the King of Kent he had converted to Christianity, although his wife and many in his court wanted to stay with the old religion. Raedwald had a Christian altar at Rendlesham and a pagan temple beside it. As well as being a successful war leader, Raedwald must have been an astute political leader. His grave would have been richer than all the others at Sutton Hoo and it was a sheer stroke of luck that it had survived unrobbed.

After the 1939 Sutton Hoo discovery, a jury met in the little wooden hut in Sutton village to decide who owned this fabulous treasure. It was awarded to the landowner, Mrs Pretty, and in an extraordinary act of generosity, she gave the treasure to the nation. It is housed today in the British Museum in London.

The helmet fragments found in Mound One at Sutton Hoo in 1939. Photograph: Wikimedia Commons user:geni

The local people had kept very quiet about their digging activities on the Sutton Hoo site in the past. They hadn't rated the objects they had found as being very important and it appears that after the 1939 publicity those objects just quietly vanished.

The site of Raedwald's burial was confirmed in 1939 but it was another 77 years before the location of his 'royal palace', the Great Hall at Rendlesham, was made public. In the 1980s John Newman walked around Rendlesham Hall and confirmed that there was a large Anglo-Saxon settlement here, but there were few details. This attracted illegal metal detectorists, 'nighthawks', who raided the countryside for profit with no concern about the historical evidence they were destroying. Eventually the owners of Rendlesham Hall realised that the fields around them were being robbed regularly. Only three nighthawks were caught, two of whom had come all the way from Essex. After this incident, the land-owner finally gave permission for an official investigation to be undertaken. Six trusted metal detectorists walked the fields in all weather, carefully recording their finds. In 2016, with further evidence from aerial photography, the position of Raedwald's Great Hall, on the edge of the Deben valley was made public.

Most of the written evidence of Raedwald and the kings of East Anglia comes from the Venerable Bede's history of England's conversion to Christianity. Raedwald's descendant Etheldreda became a devoted Christian. She was married twice, refused to have anything to do with her husbands, and retired to the monastery that she founded at Ely. The Church recognised her pious life and made her a saint.

During the reign of King Edgar (944–975), Ely Abbey was given land that it was claimed had been owned by the kings of East Anglia. Edgar granted to the Abbey the Manor of Kingston and the lands of Ubebrycg on the banks of the Deben. This was later expanded into the Liberty of St Etheldreda, a self-governing group of villages ruled over by Ely Abbey which used the income to finance the building of Ely Cathedral. The Liberty was administered from the ancient local centre at Melton. For a long time, the area was dominated by Melton.

Woodbridge became a market centre for the surrounding villages

Archaeologists digging near the Raven's Nest Field in Bawdsey, 2017. They appear to have found a medieval industrial site at the head of a creek connected to Bawdsey Fleet. Presumably this would have been part of the port of Gosford.

when, in the 1100s, Ernaldus Rufus founded a small Augustinian Canon Priory near Market Hill, where monks wore black habits. This religious body acquired the right to hold a market at Woodbridge and this no doubt attracted people to the settlement.

Everyone thinks that Woodbridge was the original port in this area but, in the medieval period, Gosford was the main port on the Deben, and a leading port on the East Coast. Gosford was not a place, but the collective name for the ships operating from both banks at the entrance of the river, at the lower end of the Deben, from King's Fleet on the Felixstowe side and Bawdsey Fleet on the eastern shore. The king gathered ships in the King's Fleet in times of war and the merchants of Bawdsey prospered in the wine trade from Gascony, and supplying Calais with beer and food. Just about all traces of Gosford's shipping activities seem to have vanished. The merchants of Bawdsey and their ships were going to European ports in the 1400s and early 1500s, but trade was moving to Woodbridge.

King's Fleet at Falkenham in 2017. This creek was part of Gosford, the medieval port on the River Deben, before it silted up.

Bawdsey Fleet, the other side of Gosford. The Bawdsey marshes were walled off in about 1575 and the water level dropped after the pumping station was built in 1962.

Woodbridge went up a gear in the time of Thomas Seckford who returned to this, his home town, after a long and successful career as solicitor to Queen Elizabeth I. The market and shipbuilding were expanding and Seckford encouraged this. He also moved the Liberty of St Etheldreda from Melton to Woodbridge although, to start with, the jail stayed in Melton and the gallows remained on Wilford Hollows Hill, near to where the golf course is now. These gallows must have been in the area that was dug away by the sand quarry just after World War II.

In 1570 Seckford built the Shire Hall, a new courtroom on the Market Hill with a corn market below it. The Shire Hall is still the administrative centre of the town, but looks as if it was squashed in, standing awkwardly between two roads. In 1884, the Victorians covered it in bricks to give the building its present appearance.

Thomas Seckford's most lasting achievement was setting up the charities in Woodbridge that were funded by his properties in Clerkenwell, London. By the time of his death in 1587, the Seckford Hospital, which housed 26 elderly single men, was up and running. The present Seckford Almshouses in Seckford Street were built in 1861. In 1886 the Seckford Dispensary was built but this petered out in the 1930s due to lack of funds.

Henry Seckford, possibly Thomas's brother, was master of the ship *Lyon* and he seized the Spanish ship *Bonaventure* in a south coast port. Since the Protestant Queen Elizabeth I was being threatened by Catholic Spain, he got away with this. But his next piece of piracy in 1592 was to seize a Venetian ship 'by mistake', for which he was fined. Piracy was looked on as being a profitable sideline for merchant ships as well as some in royal service and, even as late as the eighteenth century, Woodbridge had at least one privateer ship.

During the Elizabethan period, London merchants came to Woodbridge to order new ships to be built of Suffolk oak from the Framlingham area. Woodbridge developed as a port because it was situated about as high up the River Deben as large ships could sail.

The town's centre for local trade was the corn market and this must have been well established when, in 1680, the steelyard was built with the ability to lift a three ton wagon to assess the exact weight. This was useful when merchants brought in corn in wagons on their way down New Street to be shipped out. At some point the building became a public house and known as 'Ye Olde Bell and Steelyard' in about 1830.

By the eighteenth century Woodbridge had become the second largest port in Suffolk. The original quays appear to have been at the bottom of Quay Street where some fifteenth century warehouses survive as houses.

The river gradually silted up and, at some time in the eighteenth century, the merchant Bass, who had owned the old Tide Mill, constructed a bank into the river with the Common Quay on one side. This later became the Ferry Dock with quays on three sides, but the growing trade required more quays. The new three-storeyed Tide Mill was part of a development started in 1793 by the merchant, Cutting who also built a new quay and The Granary.

Upriver and round the bend from the Tide Mill, lime kilns were built on the quay on reclaimed land and this became Hart's Dock. On the upriver side of the Lime Kiln Quay, Sun Wharf dock, named after a public house on the main road, was constructed. Downriver, there had been the small Lord's Dock near the Woodbridge Boatyard, but this was walled off and a new jetty built so that coal ships didn't have the problems of going up Hart's Dock and Sun Wharf. As Norwegian timber ships had trouble getting up to the Pan (now Robertsons Barge Dock), part of their cargo was discharged into two lighters at Kyson Point and then rowed upriver.

The demand for commercial outlets saw more quays being constructed. The Melton Dock was built in about 1794 for trading sloops to bring in material to the new Lime Kiln Quay. This dock is now under the Melton boatyard, where Simon Skeet's workshop stands. Later a malt house was built here and a wooden granary on stilts followed by a large maltings, holding about a thousand tons. In about 1846 the New Quay, further down the river, was constructed as an outlet for brickfields which were later replaced by the large Melton

These houses in Waterside Road were probably originally fifteenth century warehouses on the quay at Woodbridge.

Hill Maltings. While Wilford Wharf, just below the road bridge, was constructed so that road-making material could be brought in for Suffolk County Council.

Large mooring posts were put up off the jetty to haul the schooners out of Lord's Dock. There were also posts from the Tide Mill all the way up to Wilford Wharf so that the barges could be hauled around the bends to speed up their progress. Normally barges only went up to Wilford Wharf on spring tides.

Because the Suffolk coast is close to Europe it has had to be defended over the centuries. A garrison was first established at Woodbridge in 1750 but, when Napoleon gained control over France there became a serious possibility his troops might land in Suffolk. In 1803, barracks covering 56 acres (22.67 hectares) were put on land near Drybridge Hill and some county roads were straightened so that troops could march at speed.

The new barracks were able to accommodate 700 cavalrymen and 4,000 infantrymen. In 1805, the 21st Light Dragoons were billeted in the barracks and a large number of old Tudor and Elizabethan houses

Woodbridge waterside in about 1770. The Ferry Dock Quay already extended out over the ooze mud and the Tudor single storey Tide Mill is still standing.

were given more fashionable Georgian fronts so that they could be let to officers. A small theatre was built to entertain them and this seems to have given its audiences a simple diet of light comedies. However, the townspeople were not impressed and complained that the theatre was 'old fashioned'. In fact, the people of this peaceful country market town loathed the task of housing the red coats. The chief amusement of these healthy young men was getting drunk and having a good scrap, habits that must have placed a severe strain on the tempers of regular church and chapel-goers. The defeat of Napoleon was greeted with enthusiasm, not because it meant the end of a tyrant, but because soldiers were no longer needed in Suffolk. The barracks were pulled down in 1815 and the material sold.

The nineteenth century saw a small group of cultured men living in Woodbridge and most of these are now forgotten outside the home town. The first of these was Bernard Barton (1784–1849) who achieved fame with his poems. This quiet Quaker was a clerk in Alexanders Bank (now Barclays) and wrote his poems in his spare time. He achieved national fame and, in 1845, Barton dined with the Prime Minister, Sir Robert Peel, at Whitehall. The following year Barton was granted a special pension by Queen Victoria.

While his poems were popular, Barton was tempted to give up work at the Bank, but both Byron and Lamb advised him against it. Neither of them were keen on his poems, but Lamb's warning of 'trust not to the public' was no doubt a fair statement.

The Quaker's Burial Ground in Turn Lane where Bernard Barton is buried.

Instead of seeking higher fame, Barton remained in Woodbridge, seldom venturing many miles away. He described himself as having 'little more locomotion than a cabbage'. He wore plain clothes and spoke in the modest language befitting a Quaker. His habits were so consistent that housewives knew that it was time to put the potatoes on to boil when they saw the respected bank clerk going home to lunch in his cottage in Cumberland Street.

Barton had many literary friends, but he was closest to Edward FitzGerald (1809–83) born at Bredfield House. 'Old Fitz' was the third son of John Purcell, who married his cousin Mary FitzGerald. After the death of Mary's father, the Purcells legally adopted the FitzGerald name and arms, and the great wealth that went with them. As well as property in Ireland, other estates they owned were Bredfield House, Boulge Hall, Wherstead Park and Nazeby.

FitzGerald lived the life of a gentleman. He moved about a great deal, but his first home was Boulge Cottage, then for 13 years he lodged over the shop of Berry the gun-maker, on Market Hill. He had Little Grange built to his own plans, but still preferred the humble rooms over the gun-maker's shop and didn't move until he had a disagreement with his landlord.

One of FitzGerald's great interests was literature and he was particularly keen on translating the classics. As a boy, he had been enlightened by Major Moor of Bealings House about the romance of the East. This retired officer of the East India Company had studied Suffolk words and archaeology. FitzGerald never visited the East, but spent many hours translating the work of the medieval poet Omar Khayyam.

These translations gained a great deal from FitzGerald's own poetic ability. His friends were interested in them and, for their benefit, he had small paperback editions printed and published. Those who read the *Rubaiyat of Omar Khayyam* were struck by its originality. Swinburne, for instance, found a copy in a second-hand bookshop in London and became enthusiastic about the translations. These slowly reached a wider public and FitzGerald's publisher was bombarded for more copies and fresh translations. The reserved gentleman of Woodbridge became known in every well read 'withdrawing' room. With their usual enthusiasm for novelties, the Americans were particularly wild about Omar Khayyam's prophesies.

FitzGerald's great passion was yachting and being on the water. He owned the schooner *Scandal* (named, he claimed, after the chief product of Woodbridge), and enjoyed sailing on the River Deben and east coast. He also took a great interest in local shipping. In 1840 he attended the launching, at Taylor's Lime Kiln Yard, of a trading schooner named after his friend Bernard Barton. At the dinner held afterwards, FitzGerald jokingly went to the other end of the room from Barton, professing that he could not sit at the same table as one about to have a schooner named after him. Barton's comment was 'if my Bard ship never gets me to the muster role of Parnassus, it will get into the shipping lists... I shall at any rate be registered at Lloyds.'

As a young man, FitzGerald had been up at Cambridge University in the same 'set' as Thackeray, Carlyle and Tennyson. On one occasion

Tennyson came to see his friend in Woodbridge. The visit was full of minor disasters including the meat being cold at Sunday dinner. However, FitzGerald took him to visit John Grout's famous stables at the back of the Bull Hotel. Grout was proud of his stud, but not particularly impressed with his visitor. FitzGerald told him afterwards that the town had been honoured by a visit from Lord Tennyson, but Grout had never heard of him. If he had been Admiral Rous of the Jockey Club or someone of importance, the honour might have been more obvious to him. Who was Tennyson anyway?

'The Queen's poet,' replied FitzGerald, stoutly.

'Dis'say,' said John Grout. 'Anyway he didn't fare to know about horses when I showed him over the stables.'

Everyone in Woodbridge was very proud of Grout. Newspapers claimed that he made the town famous 'as a place where horses and riding horses of the finest stamp could be procured'. Horse dealer Grout was the son of a Kettleburgh farmer who had 'gone bust' at the time of the Repeal of the Corn Laws. He had worked as a groom at several inns and then for Squire Sheppard of Campsea Ashe, before becoming landlord of the Bull Hotel. Seven years before his death in 1887, Grout told a friend that he had sold £100,000 worth of horses in a year. The friend quickly calculated that he must have taken at least 10 per cent profit. 'Aye,' retorted Grout, 'but there are many losses, very heavy expenses.'

In an age when horses were the main source of transport, local pride saw Grout of Woodbridge in the same terms as Ford of Dagenham. He would be remembered. But Fitzgerald? Well, he was a quiet old gentleman who had a boat on the river and kept himself to himself. Few in the town even knew he wrote, let alone dreamt that the town would be noted by future generations for the place where he had lived.

After Barton's death, FitzGerald married his daughter Lucy. This was not a love match; the couple were middle-aged and FitzGerald was beguiled into believing that this was the way to care for his old friend's daughter. Unfortunately she tried to force him to conform to dressing for dinner and sending out visiting cards. FitzGerald hated display and the couple soon parted. He remained aloof and spent the rest of his life appreciating the beauty of East Anglia. He mixed only with a little group of cultured men who referred to themselves as the 'Wits of Woodbridge'. This group regularly dined in style with a great deal of food and drink. They had consisted of Barton, The Rev Crabbe (grandson of the Aldeburgh poet), Captain Brook of Ufford Park, and the lawyer and artist Thomas Churchyard (1798–1865).

Churchyard practised law in the local courts, but his real interest was painting. A capable artist, his work is a poetic record of Victorian Woodbridge, rural and slow-moving, but a happy place to live.

Although Churchyard did some oil paintings, most of his work was in watercolours, dashed off at great speed as if they were studies of something to be finished later. He bought and enjoyed paintings by John Constable and thus developed something of his style of landscape painting. Churchyard is now seen as being a link between Constable and the later nineteenth century painters, the Smythe brothers, G.T. Rope and many others.

Churchyard had an overwhelming desire to paint but, in 1832, his financial affairs collapsed and there was a sale of his work and belongings. Then married with five children – four girls and a boy – he left the district, possibly to try his luck in London. However, he returned to live in Seckford Street (then Well Street) and, for the last thirty years of his life, he lived in Cumberland Street.

Churchyard used his ability and knowledge of the law to defend the underdog, often for no fee. He was something of a champion of the poor and disliked the 'game preservers', on their great estates with small armies of gamekeepers. He delighted in seeing the local poachers walking down the steps of the Shire Hall after the case against them had collapsed. This success had a strange reward because the agent of the Marquis of Hertford, who had a large estate near Orford and was one of the largest 'game preservers' persuaded his employer to pay Churchyard a retainer as the prosecuting solicitor in all their game and poaching cases. Churchyard was never successful enough to turn down this good offer and it was bad news for the poachers.

Perhaps Churchyard was something of a poacher himself. He certainly enjoyed a day's rough shooting out with his dog and a gun. On one occasion he took his favourite retriever into the shop of the Quaker confectioner, Barritt. Churchyard didn't notice that his dog had eaten a number of sausage rolls. A few days later Barritt was standing in his shop doorway when Churchyard came walking past and Barritt told him that a dog had eaten some of his sausage rolls.

'Oh,' said Churchyard, 'you can recover from the owner of the dog.'

'Then hand over eighteen pence,' cried the Quaker, 'because the dog was yours!'

'Very well,' said the quick-witted man of the law, 'I charge you six shillings and eight pence for my advice, so that the balance due to me is five shillings and eight pence.'

# THREE

# The Grand Old Days

Woodbridge was very much a market-place for the villages around it. Thursday used to be the day when farmers came in to sell grain at the Corn Exchange and on alternate Thursdays cattle came in to be sold on Market Hill. All this trade moved to Ipswich, but there was still a chicken auction on Market Hill in the late 1920s. The weekly stallholders' market was revived in about 1972.

Woodbridge was the marketplace for two distinctly different areas, with the A12 road being their border. To the west of the road lay High or Heavyland Suffolk, a wheat-growing area with huge Tudor farmhouses and little villages nestling in valleys between cultivated fields. To the east lay the sand lands and coastal villages. This was a very different county with few trees and plenty of wide open heath-land known as the Sandlings. On slightly better land, there were ploughed fields. The Sandlings were swept by bitterly cold winds, particularly east winds in the spring.

In the past, the Sandlings had huge flocks of sheep grazing on the heaths, but when Australia and New Zealand started exporting wool and sheep meat into England, the Sandlings flocks could not compete. The 'Sheep Walks' of East Suffolk were abandoned and left wild until after World War II.

The first irrigation appeared in East Suffolk in 1953 when James Mann and Norman Simper bought field sprinklers to wash salt water out of the land after the East Coast Flood the previous February. They soon realised that irrigation would be much more useful for improving arable crops.

East Suffolk has its own unique maritime climate caused by the

The Easter Fair on Market Hill, Woodbridge, 2013. Market Hill had been the place where crops and livestock were sold.

tidal estuaries. This salty atmosphere reduces the impact of winter frosts. In the Sandlings the growing season starts, in spite of the cold winds, two weeks earlier than in the rest of East Anglia and lasts about a week longer in the autumn. Irrigation coupled with the knowledge of the local climate kicked off a complete change in farming methods and vegetables, grown for the supermarkets, became the important crops.

When a friend took me for a flight over the Sandlings on a cold winter's afternoon I was amazed at the number of irrigation reservoirs that were glinting in the sunlight all along the Suffolk coast. In 1984 I was approached by a vegetable packer from the Fens to rent out land to grow early crops for the supermarkets. At this time the Sandlings effectively became part of the Fens, providing much needed food for the urban population.

The first golden era of farming in Suffolk, though, had been in Tudor times when small individual farms replaced the unproductive common land. While sheep and wheat were steadily abandoned on the coast, one crop, barley for malting, helped to sustain local farms. Huge new red brick maltings appeared all over East Suffolk to supply the London, Ipswich and Norwich brewers.

The account books of Heavyland farmers, the Ling family at Otley Hall, covering the period from 1745 to 1845, had me beaten to start with until I realised that they had been started at both ends and worked towards the middle. These records contained bills, sales, settlements with workers, harvest contracts and parish poor rates. Every village had to maintain its own poor so that farmers and employers tended to have as many workers as possible to keep the poor rates down.

The overall impression of the Ling accounts is that for the people in the village very little changed and the pattern of agriculture stayed much the same. Everything was done by hand with horses under-taking the hauling work. The whole village moved at the speed of a horse.

After harvest, the sheaves of corn were taken into the wooden barn, which was such a feature of rural Suffolk, and stacked up on each side of the central threshing floor. In the winter the men started the backbreaking work of hitting the sheaves on the floor to shake out the grain. Corn was threshed by hand with a flail (called a 'stick and half' in Suffolk) on the barn floor. The doors were kept open so that the dust blew out.

In the late 1700s William Ling usually employed his farm workers on a daily basis, in 'piecework,' where they were paid so much for each task. His men got a shilling (ten pence) an acre for hand-scything barley in the harvest; for threshing with a flail, they earnt six and a half pence for each 'cum' (coomb) of barley, six pence for oats, and the princely sum of one shilling and one pence for wheat.

At the time of the Napoleonic Wars, prices seem to have doubled. Boys were employed to fill the spaces left by the men who were away fighting. The boy Hammond worked seven days a week scaring rooks and crows off the corn for three shillings and six pence. Hammond must have tramped around the cornfields of Otley Hall on the spring corn 'a-shouting and a-hollering fit to bust'. There was little rest for boys or crows for, as Hammond chased the crows off, the boy Sam on the next farm chased them back again.

Farmers ploughed up more and more 'waste land' until prices collapsed after the Corn Laws were removed. As the value of the pound was high, cheap foreign grain flooded into the ports and there was considerable poverty in the villages right up to World War I.

Most villages saw their population drop steadily through the long Victorian agricultural depression. In 1844 Alderton, a large village in the Sandlings, had 620 people living there. However forty years later the number had fallen by 100, and by 1921 it had gone down to 426.

In 1879 there was a very bad harvest; what a dismal year it must have been for the countrymen. Three quarters of the hay and clover, food for the horses, was ruined by rain, and floods had carried away some of the crops on the low land. At Framlingham, passengers had to be taken to and from the station by rowing boat.

After months of wet weather, the harvest began. A wet harvest is something that has to be experienced to be understood. Days rolled by with nothing getting done, the corn was flattened by rain and the ears began to drop off. At last, the weather broke and out everyone went to the fields – but not for long. Black clouds soon built up in the sky and soon more rain fell. Another day had slipped by.

The newspapers also recorded bad news. The British troops were fighting for control over Afghanistan without success. In the middle of September there were a few fine days and all that was left of the corn harvest was gathered in. At 9am on 19th September a thunderstorm broke out, killing a cow on Dunningworth Hall marshes and another belonging to Mr Chaplin at Sudbourne. Richard Rope of Sudbourne wanted to get his bullocks back from the Leiston marshes, but was delayed for several days because the roads were flooded. Luckily he managed to get them home and into the yard before the bad storms of 23rd and 24th September.

Many people left the villages in search of work. They often walked into Woodbridge or travelled to Ipswich where the expanding industries needed hard-working county people. Some went to the capital, mostly to encounter worse poverty in the slums of East London. A few more enterprising people found their way to Western Canada.

World War I brought a mini-boom to rural East Anglia, but in 1921 cereal prices collapsed once more and farmers who had bought land at high prices during the wartime boom were bankrupted. The public had no sympathy, according to letters to the *East Anglian Daily Times*. They said that it was their own fault for growing the wrong sort of wheat.

It is not surprising that the older generation were religious, even if there was no love lost between church and chapel-goers. In the second half of the nineteenth century, Mr Leggett, who farmed with his father at Bucks Hall, Rishangles, and later on his own at Worlingworth, kept diaries that reveal much about daily life. He and his family went to church every Sunday and once, during a wet spring drilling, he left work at two o'clock on a fine day to go and hear a Mr Hamilton preach. A month later, he again left work to visit the church, this time to give bread away to the poor. A few days later, he drove his daughters into Eye to have their hair cut and to give a cheque to a Mr Warner, to be invested. Mr Leggett's diaries also reveal that he was fond of shooting. The fact that he and his neighbours had much pleasure this way was the true hallmark of the East Anglian yeomen. One September they shot all day at Garnham's and only bagged one bird.

The turn-of-the-century Relief of the Siege of Ladysmith, during the Boer War, is mentioned alongside such remarks as 'killed eight pigs for London'. Pig killing was a monthly event on the farm, and I doubt if anybody went hungry in Mr Leggett's household. Of course, it was much cheaper to eat food produced at home. Imagine being obliged to pay 'four shillings and thru pence' for 6lbs of beef, as Mr Leggett did one day in Framlingham!

Entertainment, apart from shooting, was very limited. The highlight of the farming year was the harvest, known as the 'horkey'. Everyone went to church and sang 'All is safely gathered in'. But the real climax was the horkey supper given by the farmer for his men and held in the farmhouse or barn.

In villages made up of small farms, everyone clubbed together. At the end of September 1885, Mr Leggett records going to Mr French's for a committee meeting of the Worlingworth Harvest Home Supper. The following Sunday they had two collections for it and raised four pounds, four shillings and a penny. The village craftsmen had their own celebration on the first Monday after Christmas – 'Schumacher' Monday, when the shoemakers all got drunk. This seems to have been a very local custom, the origin of which is lost.

During the whole of the nineteenth century, estates tended to get larger and the ownership of land fell into fewer hands. Although some of the older and smaller estate owners lived off the rents of their land, most of the larger ones had money invested in industry and used the returns from this to improve their estates and maintain their high style of living.

A man who went to a London estate agency wanting to buy a farm was asked what sort of farm he wanted – was it for hunting, shooting or fishing? With agriculture in a decline, the countryside had become the rich man's playground. In East Anglia, the sporting gentry made the pheasant the king of the countryside. The Victorians developed shooting with the same drive as they used to conquer the world, and what startling results they achieved. Prince Frederick Duleep Singh's 17,000 acre Elveden Estate recorded taking an 81,877 bag in one season, of which 58,140 were rabbits. On one shoot, eight guns are reputed to have shot 2,000 game birds in a day. I am inclined to believe that a little bragging went on concerning the number of game taken on rival estates. However, writers of that time defended shooting. 'Why,' they cried, 'land that could be let for sheep walks at two shillings and sixpence an acre could be let for shooting at a pound an acre!' Farming had sunk very low indeed.

In order to achieve the best results, game preservers remodelled their estates. It is no exaggeration to say that the habits of pheasants have dictated the East Anglian landscape. Tree-planting became the rage, although FitzGerald complained bitterly that the 'new-fangled race of squires' were cutting down the old woods and banks that bred violets in his childhood. This had probably been done simply to satisfy the age-old demand for oak.

Lord Rendlesham owned some of the poorest land in the Sandlings and undertook the most ambitious forestry planting in the district. He started a nursery for rearing seedlings at Chillesford and planted what was known as Tangham Forest, though unfortunately the trees were destroyed by fire. Later, in the 1920s, the Forestry Commission bought the land and re-established planting there to give us Tunstall and Rendlesham forests. The young trees were drawn from the original nursery beside the Orford Road.

The Orwell Park Estate, which comprised most of the land in the peninsula between the Orwell and Deben estuaries, also went in for forestry, particularly on the very light land at Nacton and Foxhall. Before passing into the hands of the Pretyman family, this estate was owned by Col. G. Tomline. He could, rightly, be called the founder of Felixstowe because he encouraged the growth of the town. The local story is that Tomline gave Harwich and Dovercourt the chance to elect him into parliament, but the people of the fashionable 'watering place' of Dovercourt declined to avail themselves of the opportunity. Tomline was not at all pleased and was tempted to believe that the little hamlet of Felixstowe, since it faced south, would make a better seaside resort than Dovercourt. He was the driving force behind many of the schemes that developed the modern town along the sea-front, in particular, bringing the railway to the town and opening Felixstowe Dock in 1887.

Another man closely connected with many schemes to develop East Suffolk was Sir Cuthbert Quilter. Born within the sound of Bow Bells, he was the grandson of Samuel Sacker Quilter who had a significant farm in Trimley. As a young man, Quilter came to Suffolk for holidays. Once, when out walking, he hitched a lift in a farm cart going towards Felixstowe Ferry. Here, he looked out across the Deben at the barren land on the north bank that marks the mouth of the estuary and thought if he ever made a fortune, there would be the place he would build a house. He did both.

Quilter became a stockbroker and the head of Quilter, Balfour & Co. At times, his financial dealings were on an international scale. In 1873, at the age of thirty-two, he left his home in Surrey, where he had commanded the 4th Surrey Rifles, and moved to East Suffolk. Here, he commissioned the building of a magnificent mansion, Bawdsey Manor. Completed in 1882, this palace by the sea cost him £25,000. Architecturally, it might be described as a cross between an Elizabethan manor house and a maharajah's palace. It was built in a style never likely to be repeated again, but it firmly established Quilter as being a country gentleman. Actually, it could be said that this industrious man had little in common with the older and more easy-going order of country estate owners. It was reputed that for every million he made, Quilter had another tower added to the Manor. There appear to be nine towers.

Quilter bought up most of the land and houses in Bawdsey and Alderton and, in 1892, all of Ramsholt. He went on to buy much of Shottisham and Sutton from Lord Rendlesham, as well as farms in Hollesley and Trimley. Like all the great Victorian landowners, he was passionate about shooting and he remodelled the countryside to suit the habits of the pheasants. When he went into Woodbridge he travelled through his own estate for the first eight miles – land he had bought with capital he had created.

Bawdsey Manor started in about 1882 with a small house on the sea front. As Sir Cuthbert Quilter's wealth grew he kept adding bits on and bought up most of the villages on the eastern side of the River Deben. The cliff gardens were made with Pulhamite, cement mixed with seashells.

The aristocracy was the ruling class and, in 1885, Quilter embarked on a political career, entering Parliament as a member for South Suffolk. He was popular in his constituency but never reached great heights in government circles. He fought a hard campaign to try and bring in a 'Pure Beer' Act. Although unsuccessful, he sought to prove his point by opening a brewery at Melton that produced pure beer. No doubt today's real ale campaigners would have approved.

Quilter rarely spoke in the House of Commons and presumably did not rise to a high position in the Liberal Party because of his bitter opposition to Gladstone's home rule policy. In 1906 he was created a baronet. Local legend credits him with having refused a knighthood three times previously. This came at the end of his political career as he'd lost his seat by 136 votes earlier that year.

He had no intention of letting the affairs of the nation pass without his thoughts making an impact. In the years after his retirement new taxes were introduced, aimed at the wealthy upper classes. Quilter saw quite correctly that this was the beginning of the end for the landed gentry. The taxes were only a fraction of the amount every large, privately owned enterprise has to pay today but Quilter felt he was being unjustly treated. He announced that the taxes had ruined him, and that he would have to sell his picture collection in order to pay them. His taste for fine art was inherited from his father who had also been a noted collector. The Quilter collection was housed at his London home in 28 South Street, Park Lane and sold at Christie's on 9 July 1909 for £87,780.

This splendid protest against taxation on earnings, forged from individual initiative, made not the slightest difference to the course of British political history. The average voter was not in the least distressed to see proud aristocrats stripped of their finery. Over half a century passed and the whole breed of wealthy men with unchallenged power became extinct, before central government began to dig deeply into the weekly packet of wage earners. By then, the principle of taxation on individual earnings had been long established. I fancy that Quilter, were he still alive, would only comment briskly, 'I told you so'.

At its peak, his Bawdsey estate reached 8,000 acres, extending along practically the whole north bank of the Deben. This was controlled by an agent and administered from the estate office at Bawdsey. Here, there were blacksmiths, wheelwrights and building tradesmen. The Forestry Department had its own nursery and an ambitious planting scheme. The well-known stud of Suffolk Punches kept at Bawdsey Hall carried off prizes at all the local shows, and the flock of Suffolk sheep won equal fame.

The estate was really Quilter's private kingdom, but he took his task of looking after the welfare of everyone on the estate very seriously. There was only one sin that could not be forgiven – poaching. If caught, a man could not expect to find another job the Bawdsey side of Wilford Bridge. A tenant farmer, who became irritated by having game eat his crops and had ignored the gamekeeper's orders to stop netting hares, was turned out. Apart from these high-handed actions, Quilter did a great deal of good. He was the first person in the area to build decent housing for workers.

Once, after passing a large group of men standing on Alderton Knoll, Quilter spoke to his agent, demanding to know what the men were doing standing about on his estate in the middle of the day. The agent explained they were out of work. Quilter set about finding a scheme to give them employment. Pits were opened on light land and the soil was sifted for flints, which were used for road-making.

One of his shepherds, Mr Last, lived with his wife in the little white weather-boarded cottage on Alderton Walk. Mrs Last claimed she was very proud of her grandchildren, so Quilter offered her a shilling for every descendant she could name, a gesture that cost him over two pounds.

He carried out much of the estate's day-to-day running himself. Once, at the turn of the century, nine corn stacks and the farm buildings at High House Farm went up in a glorious blaze. No-one knew how the fire had started, but two points were clear – the tenant's corn stacks were exceptionally well insured, but the landlord's farm buildings were not. Quilter pretty soon went round to investigate.

'I just don't know what started it, Sir,' said the farmer, standing respect-
fully, with cap in hand. 'I just don't rightly know what I'm gonna do,
come next rent day. All my corn stacks are burn to the ground.'

Sir Cuthbert Quilter cut him short, demanding to know if he used
a mirror to shave with.

'Why, yes Sir, that I do.'

'Then,' said Quilter crisply, 'tomorrow morning you will meet the
man who started that fire.'

For all his brilliance and forceful personality, there were two difficulties he could not overcome. One was the sea – which in spite of
£120,000 and the skill of Dutch engineers, he could not stop from
slowly encroaching on his estate. The other was the Reverend Allott
Tighe-Gregory who, from 1848 to 1911, held the living of Bawdsey
church. Quite what the original disagreements were about have been
lost in the mist of time. It appears that the aged reverend, who used to
wear a shawl, held the living until he was well over ninety. He was one
of those individuals who stubbornly refused to bow to pressure from
strong authority. Quilter loathed him and did everything in his power
to get Tighe-Gregory out. Quilter was not a man to be crossed. Once,
he won his point with the local education body by building another
school, opposite the Star Inn, and ordering that all the children in the
village should go there. He tried the same tactics with Tighe-Gregory
and ordered all the tenants to go down to Bawdsey Manor Chapel.
However the Bawdsey parishioners stayed loyal to their aged parson
and used to carry him into church on a chair.

Quilter had built his Bawdsey Manor on a cliff top with wonderful
views of the entrance of the Deben, but to make it more private,
without any permission, he had faggots laid on the marshes and a
new road built for the public. Tighe-Gregory continued to be driven
along the old road, which didn't please Quilter.

The Reverend Tighe-Gregory also held the living of Ramsholt
church. He used to cycle there on his three-wheeled bicycle every
week and hold a very short service. On one occasion, Quilter took
some friends upriver on his steam yacht *Peridot*, then walked across

After Quilter's famous dispute with the Rev Tighe-Gregory he built a 'tin tabernacle' chapel in the grounds of Bawdsey Manor and ordered his tenants to attend services there. However most of the parishioners continued to go to Bawdsey Church and used to carry the aged Tighe-Gregory into church on a 'litter'.

the Dock Marshes to church, but they arrived there just in time to find the parson shutting up the church. Quilter demanded the church be opened and insisted Tighe-Gregory was to hold another service, but the Reverend simply told Quilter he should be more punctual next time, climbed on his three-wheeler and pedalled off.

Life at Bawdsey Manor was exceptionally rigid. Younger members of the household were not expected to speak to their elders unless they were spoken to first. This rule wasn't made for servants, but for actual members of the family.

Winter shoots were the great social events. Bawdsey Estate apparently used to be shot by only four 'guns', each having two guns and a loader. They are credited with often taking 400 pheasants at one stand. To achieve this, the sky above the 'guns' must have gone black with flying birds.

A horse drawn coach loading on to the Bawdsey steam chain ferry, c. 1900.

Yet above all, Quilter loved the sea and was commodore of the Royal Harwich Yacht Club from 1879–1909. Yachting was then a popular pastime, with the great centres on the south coast, but as a pleasure sport it was comparatively unknown in Suffolk. The older country pursuits were the ruling passion of the wealthy. Parks were very popular. Notably, Sudbourne Hall stood surrounded by over 500 acres of parkland, and there must have been talk about Ashe High House, near Wickham Market. The mansion that bore the Ashe High House name has been demolished, but in its heyday the house sat amidst 144 acres of parkland, which was home to a famous deer herd. The estate changed hands from the Sheppards to the Lowther family while Quilter was still adding to his own empire. Bawdsey Manor had no park but it did have a wonderful view of the Deben flowing out into the North Sea.

Once, while on a cruise, Quilter's outspoken manner ran him into deep water. He had an argument with an American and expressed views on the United States that were not complimentary. The American contacted the New York Press and relayed Quilter's comments, describing them as representative of a member of the House of Commons. The subsequent rumpus eventually got into the London papers. The Anglo-American relationship was a tricky subject, but the Victorians sadly underestimated the resources and determination of the young America. Perhaps there were some justifications, for Great Britain at that time had controlling influence over at least half the world's surface, while the Americans were still brutally colonising at the expense of the Native Americans.

One of Quilter's maritime endeavours was the instigation of the Bawdsey-Felixstowe steam ferry. This may have been prompted by the acquisition of Laurel Farm, Felixstowe, on the south bank. Also, when the tide was not suitable to reach Woodbridge, Quilter was then able to cross the river and use Felixstowe station. The ferry consisted of two vessels that ran on chains laid across the riverbed because of the very strong tide in the Deben entrance. In spite of this being well patronised, especially in the summer, 'the bridges' as they were referred to, ran at a loss and finally petered out in the 1920s.

An even more ambitious scheme was to transform the quiet country village of Bawdsey into Bawdsey-on-Sea, the fashionable resort of the East Coast. This had already happened to Felixstowe, when the little village around the Church of St Peter and St Paul was pushed into the background as the Edwardian town mushroomed up along the sea-front. The Coastal Development Corporation built a new half-mile-long pier in 1904, complete with an electric tramway. The place was a real boom town, although the large, genteel hotels along the front tried to give the image of old-fashioned respectability. The town had reached the status of an urban district by 1894, but history did not repeat itself across the water at Bawdsey.

Quilter collapsed and died suddenly at Bawdsey in November of 1911 at the age of seventy. His estate had become a well-run community, almost a miniature welfare state; his 'good and faithful' estate workers could look forward to protection in their old age and sickness. It differed from the present form of national security in that only the 'good and faithful' received this blessing. The work-shy, the dishonest and the poacher were not encouraged to stop in the district. Nor was there any nonsense about democracy; Quilter's decision was final. Everyone else was required to keep their opinions to themselves.

In more recent years, after the two world wars, social progress has made it very difficult for an individual to exercise the level of autocracy enjoyed by Quilter – unless he or she has the backing of some powerful organisation or belongs to the new class of super-rich. When he had Bawdsey Manor built, Quilter had the main road re-routed so as not to spoil his view.

Though the most famous of Quilter's family of seven was the composer Roger Quilter (1877–1953). Bawdsey Estate, the baronetcy and the bulk of the fortune was inherited by the eldest son, Sir W Cuthbert Quilter (1873–1952), who lived the life of a country gentleman amidst a slowly crumbling estate.

In the agricultural depression of the inter-war years, farm rents could not support the grand scale the estate had been designed to run on. There was by that time a small army of estate workers. The duty of keeping up employment in villages on the estate was still taken seriously and retired retainers were found free housing – no one was turned away. This created a great personal loyalty to the Quilter family but, in the long run, it proved financially exhausting. Sir W. Cuthbert Quilter had inherited such a vast wealth and benevolent power that he must have found it almost impossible to realise the money could ever be spent.

A great deal was spent on sea defences and planting up the eastern shore of the Deben with woods for pheasants as shooting was a favourited pastime of Quilter. This planting was performed by the local men and women who were out of work and drastically chang-ed the countryside from open fields to today's wooded landscape. Bawdsey Manor was the first sacrifice. Apart from employing suffi-cient staff to maintain this small-scale palace (not to have maintained it properly was unthinkable), there was also the constant problem of the encroaching sea. Even after the thousands of pounds the Quilters devoted to shore defences, the short, grey waves of the North Sea still tried to gnaw it away from the Sandlings peninsula. And still today, the sea defences have to receive regular attention if the age-old battle is to be won.

The Bawdsey Estate eventually succumbed to the ravages of death duties. The grandson of the 'right old Sir Cuthbert' Quilter, Sir Raymond Quilter (1902–59) was the last man to head the estate whilst it was intact in its original form. Sir Raymond was a second son,

**The second Sir Cuthbert Quilter at a pheasant shoot with his wife Lady Gwendolyn.**

brought up to believe that he would have to make his own way in the world, but his elder brother died and the younger brother eventually inherited. Sir Raymond had the same dynamic personality as his grandfather and although he was in many ways a very sensitive man, he possessed the courage of a lion. In his youth, he had his own plane and used to make parachute jumps over Felixstowe sea front to amuse the summer visitors. The parachute was then in its infancy. Although these daredevil escapades did not altogether meet with approval from Bawdsey Manor, he later began the GQ Parachutes & Co at Woking in Surrey, having rightly anticipated that the parachute would play an important part in the Second World War.

What the Quilter domain may have lost in size, Sir Raymond made up for in originality. His home was the chauffeur's cottage at Methersgate Hall. His own airfield was on the edge of Sutton Walks,

Bawdsey Manor when it was RAF Bawdsey Radar Station, in 1953.

and his plane is referred to as being 'the best radio-equipped private plane in Britain'. While 'in residence' at London's Dorchester Hotel, he had his own standard, a golden pheasant on a red background, flying alongside the Union Jack.

The Quilter Estate broke up slowly. Bawdsey Manor was sold to the government in 1936, and it was here that a team headed by Sir Robert Watson-Watt developed radar. This was the first operational radar station in the world. It became part of the Chain Home Stations that played a vital part in the Battle of Britain. After RAF Bawdsey Radar Station closed in 1976, the Manor reopened as RAF Bawdsey with ground to air Bloodhound missiles stationed there. When the Cold War ended, the RAF withdrew in 1990. The Quilter estate continued to be sold – with Bawdsey and Alderton going in 1953, Ramsholt and Shottisham in 1959, and finally Sutton was sold in 2018.

FOUR

# Men of the Country

To attempt to define a countryman is a difficult task. The term is only a loose one connected with an attitude of mind rather than being applied to everyone living in a rural area. Basically, the countryman is part of the country. His life is set against a background in which nearly everything is growing or living and not being manufactured by any skills devised by his fellow human beings. He sees nature at close quarters and is not over-awed by it. He does not get excited about preserving wildlife because he is too often in direct competition with it and knows its true force and ability to survive.

His skills are unsophisticated, but nevertheless require an alert mind. Above all, he takes pride in his achievements, whether it is high yielding crops or healthy animals. He can never afford to relax his attention if these results are to be obtained. The weather with all its fickle habits and ever-present diseases are formidable foes, always against him. He has to struggle hard to make sure the seeds he plants will flourish. Countless forms of wildlife – rabbits, pigeons, insects and the rest – could destroy everything and leave him with nothing in return for his labours. It is simply a case of survival of the fittest, and the countryman has to be constantly on his guard.

It's a pity that more countrymen have not written. True, rural England has had its defenders, but all too often the country is portrayed through the eyes of townsmen. Villages emerge through a romantic haze, portrayed as oases of peace and basic well-being. Above all, there is this curious opinion that life moves slower, but in the country the four seasons come in succession and nothing will stop them. If crops are not planted at the right time, they will not grow.

'Loader' Miller of Hollesley, on Ramsholt Lodge Farm, rabbit catching with a polecat in 1968. Although the myxomatosis disease had killed most of the rabbits in 1953, numbers had increased again so that two men spent most of the winter on that 600 acre farm attempting to control the rabbit population.

A constant deadline has to be met. Political upheavals can shelve or ruin any system connected with manufacturing, or upset the laws of supply and demand, but no one has yet succeeded in completely halting nature for a single day, although the human race has tried some disastrous methods to try and change the course of its destiny.

One point about countrymen is certain; they were far more numerous in the past. What a tough old crowd they were, labouring away, taking immense pride in everything they did. It didn't matter whether it was ploughing, hedging or ditching, it all had to be done 'exact' to meet with their approval. All this gave them a great deal of satisfaction, but little financial return. The amount one man could do by hand was so limited that they could not get high returns for their labours. Their pleasures in life had to be simple and organised on a very local basis, like attending the small markets and fairs.

An incident alleged to have taken place at Parham Fair in 1764, was of the man who exchanged his wife for an ox. The deal was made with a grazier, and the wife was apparently quite willing. She was handed over the next day, complete with a new halter, in return for the ox, which the man sold the following day for five guineas. This has the ring of a real country tale, spread by word of mouth until someone wrote it down. The report, made in all seriousness, was no doubt meant to fix a price on a woman's value.

The fairs were business gatherings but they played such a great part in the social life of the district that in time they were held purely for amusement. In Dunningworth, now part of Tunstall, the fair survived while the village vanished. At one time there had been a church, but this had fallen into decay by the sixteenth century, whereas the annual horse fair, held on the strip of ground in front of Dunningworth Hall, remained a regular event right up to 1912. There would have been no auctioneer at Dunningworth Fair, with bargains struck between individuals. This old practice still exists in parts of Ireland, but in Suffolk men are no longer prepared to spend the whole day haggling over the sale of one animal.

Melton Lamb Sale, held every spring on what was then a meadow beside the church, was an annual one-day auction of sheep which

Frank Ling with the Suffolk horses
Boxer and Prince at a ploughing
match held at Norman Simper's Fir
Tree Farm, Blaxhall in 1938.

came mainly from the Sandlings. Shepherds and their dogs set off
in the early hours of the morning to walk their 'ships' in. This sale
survived the Second World War.

Woodbridge Fair, at one time held on Fen Meadow, took place on
Easter Monday. By 1875 it was no longer referred to as a fair, but rather
'what used to be a fair' as it was already developing into a horse show.
By the beginning of this century it had become well known for the
'turn out' of prime Suffolk Punches.

One Blaxhall man made a living travelling round the fairs and

fighting for money. This sport, if it can be called that, lasted long after prize fighting was abolished. The dodge was to get the crowd gathered around and then challenge someone to a fight. A cap was tossed on the ground and the crowd threw money into it. The winner of the fight took the cap money. Hard old days! In the nineteenth century, countrymen were certainly tough and, at times, downright brutal.

In the Saxmundham area, the gentlemen got together and formed the Association for the Protection of Property in the hundred of Plomesgate. This organisation paid ten part-time peace officers. Sir

Robert Peel's stout-hatted Bobbies were not established until 1829, and then only in London. In the Plomesgate Association Report for 1836, we learn something of the crime and punishment of the day. At Saxmundham, John Boom stole an ox-hide and calfskin from Samuel Flick and was sentenced to a month's imprisonment. Robert Button took several trusses of hay from the Kelsale rector and got six months hard labour. In another Kelsale incident, John Barker stole a quarter of barley and was sent for seven years transportation, while a man caught stealing at Leiston was transported for life.

Sheep stealing was a crime of the worst order and woe betide anyone who was caught. Simon Potsford, of Wickham Market, was accused of the theft of a sheep at Simon's Cross – from where he was dragged down Draghards Hill to a wood, now known as Potsford Wood, and hanged. The post still stands. Whether or not he stole a sheep in the first place, we shall never know. Perhaps he was a young man driven to steal to feed his wife and family. Unluckily, he was caught, and his sad and violent end made its mark on others.

The Plomesgate Association congratulated its members for finding more employment for the labouring classes. They said the achievement '...must tend to diminish crime. Generally speaking, persons who live in idleness and have thus opportunity to organise themselves can lay plans with less probability of being detected.'

There was some justification for the lawless habits of the people in those far-off days. The real root of the trouble was that employment was nearly always arranged as piecework, and at certain times of the year, particularly in the winter months, there were more men in the villages than there was work for. Later, a regular weekly wage basis was established, but farms and village industries still could not employ everyone born in the area. At least a man could go to the town and get work; industry was expanding and badly needed manpower.

At one time, villages were almost self-supporting, with at least a third of their population being craftsmen. The villages that bordered either the sea or an estuary provided the purely local occupation of 'marshmen'. The marshes under their care were formed on land reclaimed from the sea, which, in spite of its name, was not bog land, but grazing. The marshes are interwoven with ditches (never called dykes in Suffolk) that usually followed what had been the channels in the 'saltings' before the river wall was constructed and the land reclaimed. This land was on the tidal side of the river or sea wall and only flooded on spring tides.

The marshman's main task was to watch the animals grazing during the summer. The most usual danger, especially during dry summers, was that animals went into the ditches looking for water and got stuck in the mud; sheep were particularly prone to drowning in this way. Also, cattle and colts (young male horses) often swam or jumped the ditches and got mixed up with another owner's stock. Since one marshman had several hundred animals, belonging to different owners, under his care, careful watch had to be kept, although stray animals could be identified for a time by the telltale grey mud on them. Since all stock, especially sheep, tend to keep moving about while grazing, marshmen did not count in ones, but in twos and threes. It made counting quicker and more accurate.

During the summer months a marshman looked after stock on a large area and had to spend much of his time walking. He alone knew where to find each of the plank bridges over the ditches. Strangers were not always welcomed in this domain in case they left gates open and mixed up stock.

In the old days, the marshmen must have been in league with the smugglers, but the later generations of marshmen worked alone most of the time. They liked it that way. For company, he would have had a dog or two, and perhaps, hovering in the clear blue sky above, there might have been a solitary skylark. Like many countrymen, they were a race of individuals not seeking the refinements of life. Solitude gave them time to think, perhaps too much time. A Hollesley marshman used to visit the Lifeboat Inn at Shingle Street very regularly. He walked boldly across the narrow bridges on his way there, but coming back, he played safe and got down on his hands and knees to cross.

After looking round the stock, the marshmen 'made up the day' cutting thistles with scythes, a laborious operation referred to as 'scumming'. The ditches were cleaned out in the winter when the vegetation had died down. This work was done on a piecework basis for a set sum per chain and was known as 'cutting and drawing'. In more recent years, Mr Bear of Waldringfield was a familiar figure in his area, working away in thigh boots with his long narrow spades.

Most farms had a place where good reeds for thatching could be cut. These were used for barns, cottages and cart sheds. Corn stacks were thatched with wheat or rye straw in the autumn and occasionally wheat straw was used to repair reed thatch, but it never lasted as long. Old thatch was often repaired by being covered with another layer; this way it could last for up to a hundred years, provided it was netted well to keep out birds and rats. A barn at Street Farm, Bucklesham had the thatch removed in 1966, and carved on a beam was 'WB Thatchy 1837' – presumably the date when it was originally thatched. Thatched cottages were popular because they were easier to keep warm but, since the water from the roofs was caught in butts, for use in the house, thatch was disliked because it made the water black and only fit for scrubbing.

The thatcher was really a craftsman, but in village society he did not rank as high as the shoemaker or tailor. However, since stacks needed to be thatched on every farm, it was a common occupation and not just the speciality of a few. In the 1890s, the thatcher's wage was often thirty shillings a week and this was certainly the highest wage earned in agriculture. Normally, the thatcher had a mate working with him who pulled and carried straw.

The ability of the ploughman was probably the country skill that was noticed most. His work was on view for everyone to see, and a ploughman who left the land uneven, or with 'hog's troughs' at the headlands, was constantly reminded of this failing by his workmates. The pride in doing a job well was the basic characteristic of the old agricultural order. It applied to all those engaged in it. A farmer was not only expected to make a livelihood from his ability to produce crops, but he was also duty bound to keep the soil 'in good heart'. Estate

George Weston of Charsfield with his wooden beam horse plough in 1962. His grandfather had bought the plough in 1905. This type of plough was used on heavy land because small wheels would have got clogged up with clay. At the end of each furrow the plough had to be lifted around for the next furrow. On heavy land they ploughed an acre a day, but in light land two acres a day were ploughed.

owners actively disliked any tenant who they thought was taking more out of the soil than he was putting back. This often meant, in their opinion, too many cash crops and not enough stock. There was a strong feeling that it was not just bad farming to try and make a maximum profit out of every acre, but it was also morally wicked. The same sort of attitude was propagated among those working on the farms. It didn't matter how long it took to do a job as long as it looked neat when it was finished. The saying was: 'a job worth doing was worth doing well'.

Working with horses came almost as second nature. A girl of ten, who started work by leading horses at Alderton in the 1860s, received sixpence a week and a shilling if she worked all seven days. While it is impossible to admire a system that used child labour to such an extent, it is possible to marvel at the stamina of the people who worked such long hours.

Matches in ploughing and drawing (making one single straight furrow) were eagerly contested. In 1868, Isaac Rowe, head horseman at Winston Green Farm, won the ploughing match in that parish and received a copper kettle as first prize. But ploughing matches were only held a few times a year. Normally ploughing was a solitary occupation in which the ploughman spent many hours walking up and down behind his team of horses. It was a slow process, constantly held up by bad weather. In that beautifully unspoilt public house, The Ship at Levington, there is an iron plaque perched on top of one of the settles, depicting two horses, a plough, the ploughman and his dog. Under the plaque is the honest prayer, 'God speed the plough' – words that must have been uttered by many an exasperated farmer. The plough in this case is the old type widely used before Ransome's (of Ipswich) YL model was introduced in 1843. Until 1965, George Western, of Park Farm, Charsfield, still had a Ransomes AS2 plough that his grandfather bought some time before he moved to that farm in 1905. This was a type much favoured on the heavy lands rather than the YL with its two wheels in front. The AS2 simply had a skid for altering the depth of the furrow. The most interesting detail of this particular plough was that it had an oak frame, making it a survivor, in design at least, of the eighteenth century.

In 1934, when the Royal Show was held at Ipswich, there were 265 Suffolk horses entered, more than double the number of any other breed in the Heavy Horse Section. To have even been attending the Royal Show, these must have been the best horses and there were still thousands more at work on the farms and in industry. By 1968 the Suffolk Punch, although not in danger of imminent extinction, had shrunk considerably in numbers. At the Suffolk Horse Society's office in Church Street, Woodbridge, there were only 250 horses still registered. The Fens had become the last area where heavy horses were still worked, although several people kept horses for showing. In Suffolk there were still a dozen studs, such as Percy Adams & Sons Ltd of Laurel Farm, Felixstowe and, just outside the county, WC Saunders of Billingford Hall, Diss, still kept outstanding teams of four, six and eight horses.

Among the nineteenth century breeders, Alfred Smith of Rendlesham, and his two sons, remained closely connected with the Suffolk Punch. Fred Smith, the Woodbridge farmer who had Kingston Hall and Barrack Farm, joined the Suffolk Horse Society in 1913. Later, he became secretary of this Society and held the office for thirty-eight years. He bequeathed six acres of land, including the jetty field, to the Woodbridge Urban District Council. His younger brother, Carlyle Smith farmed Sutton Hall and was a Suffolk horse breeder on a smaller scale. Like most significant farmers of that day, he had cast iron plates made to go on the sides of his wagons, bearing his name and address.

The showing of animals played a leading part in a countryman's life. These events made it worthwhile to keep the animals in prime condition. One of the early pioneers of show organisation was the Victorian auctioneer, Robert Bond. He held the office of secretary to the Suffolk Agricultural Association for half a century and piloted its main function, the Suffolk Show, through many of its early difficulties. Born in 1827, Robert Bond was the son of a tenant farmer on the Hurts Hall Estate at Sternfield. He may well have attended the first show at Wickham Market in 1832, for his father had taken a farm in the neighbouring village of Hacheston the previous year. Mr Bond senior wanted his son to acquire as much insight into the business life of farming as possible. There were no agricultural colleges or institutes, so young Bond was encouraged to spend as much time as he could with the land agent Cornelius Welton.

Welton was the first secretary of the Suffolk Agricultural Association which was formed at the White Hart Hotel, Wickham Market, in 1831. Bond accompanied him on his rounds and helped with the valuation of large farms in the district, such as Butley Abbey and Chillesford Lodge. These visits with Welton left a deep impression on Bond, particularly the way local sales were conducted – the waste of time was enormous. Often a dealer and farmer would spend all day haggling over the sale of one cow, and then go home without striking a bargain. Spirits and wines were plied on bullock, sheep and wool buyers in the hopes of softening their hearts. These frivolities took were so prolonged that there was little time left for the actual sale, and markets had the reputation for being drunken orgies.

Bond took over the management of his father's land at Stern-field in his early twenties. His hobby became shooting, and for three seasons he had the benefit of this for free at the 3,000 acre Hurts Hall Estate. Here, he organised ploughing matches and furrow drawing competitions. These were among the early events arranged by the Suffolk Agricultural Association.

Early in the nineteenth century, farm horsemen and their families lived on a diet of dumplings, cheese made with skimmed milk and sour, or sharp beer. Although living conditions had improved slightly during Bond's lifetime, the average horseman would only have earned sixteen shillings a week. Few went hungry, but this amount did not allow for a very extravagant mode of life. A typical prize given at the Suffolk Show during this time was awarded to 'the labourer who, without receiving parish relief, had brought up the most children whom had lived more than one year'.

When the repeal of the Corn Laws started to have an effect on arable farming, the Bond family went out of business. Mr Bond senior found a position as agent for Sir Fitzroy Kelly at Chantry, Ipswich, and his son became agent at Thorrington Hall, for Colonel Benacre. To be thrown out of farming was a jolt few men got over, but luck was on young Bond's side. The following year, he was offered, and took, the tenancy of Kentwell Hall, a 500 acre farm at Long Melford (and now a fine place to visit to see the re-creation of Elizabethan family and farm life, including Suffolk Punches). Sound judgement and enthusiasm soon had him firmly established in farming once more. His abilities did not go unnoticed for, in 1857, he was elected secretary of the Suffolk Agricultural Association and it was largely due to his drive and energy that the Suffolk Show continued to develop successfully.

The East and West Suffolk Shows had amalgamated two years before Bond became secretary, but the show still had many difficulties to overcome. Cattle breeders had to be persuaded to send their stock. Even when they were in the show ring, farmers often withdrew their animals if it looked as if they were not going to win prize money. There was a protest lodged against nearly every cup winner. These situations called for a man with enormous tact who could stand firm when the need arose, and Bond did not lack personal courage. In an Ipswich election campaign he once rode into a mob, was knocked off his horse and marked on his forehead for life.

The first mechanised exhibition at the Suffolk Show was at Framlingham in 1860 when steam ploughing made its debut. The show received much better support after shelter had been provided for livestock and after the various breed societies had fixed the type classifications.

East Anglian farmers were very conscious of the lack of a good local breed of cattle. Bond made at least one visit to Denmark in search of better stock to help progressive farmers improve the Red Poll. This breed is descended from the Anglo-Saxon red cattle; its most obvious characteristic is that it has no horns, hence the name 'polled'. They were also noted for their milk yield. When Arthur Young surveyed Suffolk in the eighteenth century, he recorded that Framlingham and the surrounding woodland area of the county, was the home of the Suffolk Polled. A very early herd belonged to Mr Moseley at Glemham Hall in the 1820s. However, there was no standard description of the breed, and there was a tremendous uproar at the Suffolk Show in 1860 when the first prize was given to an undoubtedly crossbred animal. Controversy went on for years, and the breed type specification was not really settled until Henry Euren compiled and published a Red Poll herd book in 1874. But it was still a further fourteen years before a breed society was founded.

Two years after becoming secretary to the Suffolk Agricultural Association, Bond married Jane Beaumont of Cranmore House, Long Melford. A year later, he combined his experience of farming and acting as a land agent, and opened two offices to sell his services as an auctioneer and valuer. He had an office in Tavern Street, Ipswich and another in King William Street, London. Six years passed before he began conducting sales of cattle, sheep and swine on the London cattle markets. His friends urged him to do the same in Suffolk. He started

Red Poll 'Kettleburgh Rosie'; the Red Poll was the
Suffolk breed of dual purpose cow that provided
both milk and beef. The breed saw its popularity
rise in Britain and export to South America in the
1920s. From *Farmer and Stockbreeder* (1889).

the Ipswich Lamb Fair in 1867, Woodbridge in 1868, Framlingham in 1869, the Ipswich Wool Fair in 1870 and both the Fat Cattle Club and the Sutton Lamb Sale in 1871. His firm became the largest of its kind in East Suffolk.

In 1902, Bond's son, W.K. Bond, was made assistant secretary of the Suffolk Agricultural Association. Although having already taken over many of his father's duties, W.K. Bond remained in this position during his father's lifetime. Thus, Robert Bond was in his eightieth year when he reached his half-century as secretary in 1906. Bond was the main instigator in turning the Suffolk Show from something akin to the scale of a village-based ploughing match, to an annual event involving several thousands of people. He set the pattern on which it still runs – although having a show operate from a permanent site is a development that no one seriously considered in his day.

⚜

The countryman's logic was a force that could solve any situation effectively, but the methods used were not for the faint hearted. A Waldringfield farmer had trouble with corn vanishing from his meal shed. Like all farmers, he waged a constant battle against vermin, but he knew by the amount of corn missing that he had a pretty large rat to deal with. He set a gin-trap on the inside of the little finger hole of the latch on the meal-shed door. This solved the problem of the missing corn for, late one night, there was a loud cry of pain and surprise as the would-be pilferer gently pushed his finger into the latch hole. Whatever the man with the crushed finger may or may not have thought of this, it made everyone very respectful of the property on that farm.

In the past, the battle for the minds of the people living in the country was completely dominated by religion. The contest was between the church and the chapel, to try to draw the largest congregations. There was a very deep gulf between those who attended the parish church and those who were members of the chapel. Suffolk had a long tradition of nonconformist worship. Although very few chapels ever converted a whole village, they gained a foothold in most, much to the disgust of the land-owning section of the community who were, almost without exception, keen supporters of the established church. The labourers and their families were also usually churchgoers, although they often found the public houses far more attractive. The chapel people were usually the middle section of the community, which included tradesmen, shopkeepers and small farmers.

The chapel people may have broken away from the Church of England, but they were not rebels. In Wales, the chapel united the people and taught them to be great orators, but in Suffolk the effect was the reverse; it encouraged people to be modest and tended to follow the old puritan line of thought. It was always part of the East Anglian character to loathe display. Village gossip was designed to cut down to size anyone who became self-opinionated, although it was just as cruel to those who tried to better themselves. The country people were practical and hard-working, but at times a little unimaginative.

In 1864, the Evangelical church at Melton was subject to an unusual act of faith. A group of primitive Methodists had a yellow brick chapel built next to somewhere called White House. The owner of this house, perhaps a regular churchgoer, sued the stewards of the chapel for blocking out the light and being a nuisance to his property. In the subsequent lawsuit, the owner of White House won the day. He argued that the chapel quite obviously kept the light out and must be pulled down. But there was another way round this order for, if the chapel could be moved five yards nearer Woodbridge, it would be the legal distance away from an adjoining property. A firm of millwrights undertook this task, but backed out at the last minute. So the chapel stewards managed to persuade a general builder, John Cook from Grundisburgh, to take on the job. Cook strapped iron bars round the building, jacked the base up, and then, with five fir trees as rollers, he moved the chapel the necessary five yards. The rolling operation took three hours and was watched by a gathering of men in stovepipe hats and women in long dresses. One man with sublime faith sat in the pulpit while the chapel was moved.

This was an unusual case. Most of these architecturally plain places of worship led very uneventful existences. Chapels were being built in large numbers from about 1860–80 and had thriving congregations up to the First World War when the number of followers gradually dropped away until, in many cases, the chapels were sold. How disappointed those early followers would be if they could see their hard-fought-for chapels being pulled down; men like Mr Squirrel who left Grundisburgh in the 1820s and went over to Sutton where he devoted his life to a Baptist mission. At first, he held services in his cottage, then he held them in a barn, but finally, before the end of his life in 1845, he achieved his aim and had a small chapel built.

In matters of charity, the established church was well in the lead, perhaps because it was established. The chapels had to spend much of their time raising money for their building programme; moreover, their members were drawn from the less affluent. In Woodbridge, St Mary's Church ran a boot club. The idea was for those 'in happier circumstances' to give money, through church collections, to subsidise boots for children from poorer homes. Miss Pulling, the club honorary secretary, arranged for the sale of nearly a hundred pairs of boots in the first nine months of 1900. But not all charity was for such a needy cause. In the same year, money was raised to provide a 'meat tea' for two hundred herdsmen in the grand marquee at the Suffolk Show. The church attenders were asked to give generously as, 'the expense will be considerable'. No doubt those hungry country boys ate everything provided.

Not everyone thought highly of charitable deeds – those receiving used to view it with mixed feelings as there were often strings attached. There is a story that a rector of Alderton used to send his gardener out every Saturday morning to give soup to the poor and aged; that is, to those poor and aged who had been to church the previous Sunday.

The church's control over education was an ancient right going back to the very roots of British history. When the church began to educate the masses, it started schools in many towns and villages on a 'voluntarily supported' basis, but there wasn't a school for everyone until the Primary Education Act in 1870. In theory, this permitted only non-denominational religious teaching in the Board schools but the church retained a strong hold. The vicar went along to the school every week and gave lessons on the scriptures. Very rarely was the chapel pastor given such an opportunity to influence the future generation.

It was Gladstone, the political leader of the nonconformists, who established education for everyone. But his failure to take it out of the hands of the church was a bitter disappointment to the chapel people, especially in rural areas where they had no alternative but to send their children to the church schools.

In an 1899 report on the Woodbridge schools, the inspector made a few observations. At the national boys' school, he found the pupils' knowledge of the Old and New Testament to be very satisfactory, with the exception of the older boys who had omitted 2 Samuel. Also, their repetition of the catechism was not up to the level expected from a town school. These unfortunate boys, who were the sole charge of the headmaster, fell into even greater disgrace over their use of the prayer book which was a lower standard again. The girls' school got off more lightly – there was only trouble over one group's repetition of the catechism – and the infants' school came dangerously near to receiving praise. Miss Kinnell and Miss Heathcote had evidently laboured hard to impart religious knowledge. But the inspector hinted that perhaps the lessons might be made a little more interesting for both teachers and children. He ended by reporting that discipline and the standard of singing was very good in all schools.

These were the days when children were taught the alphabet, and then they learned to say it backwards at speed – all good practice and it helped to fill in the time. History lessons relied on chanting the dates of the reigns of the kings of England. Although the system may not have helped people to understand the problems around them, this indoctrination of young minds certainly worked. What they were taught, stuck. Even now, there are members of the older generation who can quote long passages from the Bible that they probably have not seen in print since their childhood.

Most of the activities of the church were expensive and there was a constant need to encourage cash donations. But the church equally encouraged other charities. In the Woodbridge parish magazine, Mrs Howey, vice-president of the Ladies Association of the Eastern Counties Idiot Asylum, was gratified to report that a house-to-house collection in Woodbridge had raised the satisfactory total of twenty pounds and two shillings. However, all was not quite so pleasing to the churchmen in the town. The theory of charity was that individuals gave according to their wealth. Woodbridge, in the opening years of this century, had become largely a residential town, a peaceful place where people could retire and live in pleasant surroundings. The church hinted that some of these (no names mentioned of course, but everyone living in the town then must have known who was being got at) were not digging deep enough into their pockets.

There were small expenditures such as the choir outing. The boys went downriver to Felixstowe and the men to Crystal Palace. There were nine men, including verger, quest man, sexton and an organ blower. The plea was to give generously and 'therefore let it be worthy of S. Mary's congregation'. Apparently, it was at the cost of ten shillings a head.

The last of the old company of change-ringers was John Fosdike, who died aged eighty-three in 1899. In the belfry at St Mary's were a number of boards that recorded the various peals they used to ring. Fosdike's campanological career was a long one. He rang a dumb-peal on the death of King William IV, then rang in the Accession of Queen Victoria and for sixty successive years he was one of the company who rang St Mary's bells on the Queen's birthday, a feat that few could have equalled – but the Woodbridge Fosdikes seemed capable of doing the unusual. Back in 1753, one Andrew Fosdike, then aged sixty-six, ran up and down the 132 steps in the 108-feet-high tower of St Mary's seven times in twenty-seven minutes. Quite why a man of that age should decide to rush up and down a church tower is not recorded, but presumably he did it for his own satisfaction.

# FIVE

# Forgotten Industries

The coprolite digging boom in the mid-Victorian period is the nearest that the River Deben area has ever got to a Gold Rush. Coprolite is fossilized animal droppings found in the Suffolk crag (which is better known for fossilized seashells) and comes to surface in the Sandlings villages. The coprolite was ground up to make phosphate and used to increase crop yields. It brought prosperity to the villages and gave employment to large numbers of people who worked on the farms in the summer and the coprolite pits in the winter. Farm wages were then 12 shillings a week while in the pits they earned a £1.

The first recorded use of Suffolk crag as a fertilizer was in 1717 when Edmund Edwards spread it on his fields at Levington. No doubt it was recognised that phosphate increased the yields on light land.

In the 1840s, William Colchester started digging for coprolite at Kyson. It was then transported by barge to his factory at Harwich to be turned into superphosphate of lime. Edward Packard also started producing fertilizer in Snape. In 1851 he moved his works to Coprolite Street near the Ipswich docks. Three years later, Packard had to move his business again, this time to Bramford, because residents in the riverside area protested about the smell of the coprolite works.

There are at least seventeen places where coprolite was extracted in Ramsholt, while Alderton and Sutton had some huge deep pits. In 1851 the steamer River Queen came round from Harwich with a party of fossil hunters. The workers used to find interesting fossils in the crag and put them to one side for sale to collectors.

Coprolite contractors walked around the fields looking for the places where seams of Suffolk crag came to the surface. They then rented the land off the landowner for a set period. The most important person was the foreman in charge of the diggings as his task was to organise the extraction of coprolite from the soil. Men from the villages were hired, mostly in the winter when there was little work on the farms, and the farmers also rented their horses and tumbrils to the contractors. After being dug out, the crag was washed to extract the nodules of coprolite, which were then carted off to be loaded on to the barges and taken to the Ipswich area for processing. In the early stages, the soil became damaged and useless for growing crops, particularly where it had been rinsed. As a result, landowners lost rent. They made demands for topsoil to be removed at the start of the process and then replaced when the seam had been worked out. There are fields behind Bawdsey Church that were worked in this way.

Without the oral tradition that has kept the memory of the coprolite era alive, it would be impossible to tell where the workings had been. At the height of the boom, the returns were so good that even part of Bawdsey Churchyard was worked in this way. There are records of cottagers allowing their gardens to be worked, earning twenty pounds – more than the houses were worth.

The landowners did very well out of the profit from coprolite. They could take £120–150 per acre in rent each year, in an age when farming might have returned one pound an acre. Some contractors did well before moving on to other business, while several foremen built new houses and even bought farms in the area. George Ling built a cottage on Ely Hill, Boyton. Over a thousand tons of coprolite were dug from fields around Waldringfield and the foreman here, John Kemp, bought the White Horse in Kirton and then a farm nearby. The boom years were probably from about 1845 to the 1870s and some Sandlings farmhouses got an update in this period. Digging continued after this but the price dropped steadily.

The labourers in the coprolite pits earned about a third more per week than they did on the farms. But shovelling by hand was hard, and they were paid as piecework. This was the time of Darwin, when the existence of prehistoric life was first discovered. Collectors who travelled around the pits bought fossils and shells and a good

Coprolite being graded at Waldringfield in about 1890 in the pit at the site of the Waldringfield Sailing Clubhouse.

collection was built up at Ipswich Museum. A leading collector, S.V. Wood, claimed he had discovered 396 species of shells in the coralline crag, of which 144 were extinct. A further 248 different species were identified in the red crag. It is believed the fossilized creatures had once lived in a warm sea 300–400 feet deep. The coprolite labourers kept the good shark's teeth they found and polished them up to hang on their watch chains as a token of their occupation.

The labourers digging near Sutton Hall once thought they had struck it rich when they discovered a hoard of gold coins on a Roman villa site. They decided not to tell their employer but knew that, if they tried to sell the gold in Woodbridge, the news would soon be all around the district. One of them was elected to go to London to sell the gold. When his train arrived in the city, he became totally lost so he decided to return home again where he handed the gold over to his employer.

The demand for phosphate fertiliser drove them to carry on digging, and they did so anywhere crag was found. It was believed that 20 feet was an economic depth to dig, but some pits were deeper – the deepest Suffolk pit, in Foxhall, was 100ft. Tunnelling in the

**The preserved coprolite pit at Sutton Knoll.**

soft crag proved impossible. Over a thousand tons were taken from the fields around the Maybush Inn at Waldringfield and the Waller family, the local landowners, had the village school built with the proceeds. In about 1860 another Waller, over on the Sutton side, built the quay at Stonner Point to ship coprolite out by barge. Other new quays were built at Methersgate, Ramsholt Dock and on the Butley River at Boyton. By the 1870s about 10,000 tons a year were being shipped to Ipswich.

Cheaper phosphate began to be imported from South America and, in about 1893, the pits (then very deep) began to be closed. In some, it looked as if the work had finished suddenly. The closing of the pits had a disastrous effect on the Sandlings villages because there was no more work in the winter. Men, women and children had worked in the pits, so many families moved to Ipswich where the expanding industries were recruiting labourers. The population of the villages fell and didn't recover until after World War II when a rise in living standards and access to cars brought people back to the countryside. Many pits were filled in and others became overgrown. There had been serious diggings around Sutton Knoll and one of the pits has since been opened for public viewing. However, this looks more like an orderly park feature than a rough and ready working pit.

There was a brief period, in the 1914–18 war, when some pits were temporarily opened and worked by machines, and several thousand tons were dug. But imports started again in 1918, and these operations quickly faded out. In the 1930s, some farmers reopened the pits and spread crag on their land as a cheap form of fertilizer. Apparently, this was done to try and kill mayweed (the presence of which often indicates a sour soil), but the spreading of crag by hand was expensive and of little use. Apart from the numerous pits that are still dotted about the Sandlings, little has survived, but in the long run it has done the district good. The surviving Ipswich factories united to form the chemical fertilizer manufacturer, Fison, Packard & Prentice. In 1942, the name was shortened to Fisons Ltd. For a period, Fisons won international success and provided a great deal of employment in East Suffolk. A research facility was opened in the village of Levington which, by a twist of fate, was the place where coprolite was first used for fertilizer. Post-war diversification into horticultural products, pharmaceuticals and scientific instruments gained Fisons a listing on the London Stock Exchange. Unfortunately, an increasing shift toward developing pharmaceuticals proved the company's downfall and Fisons suffered a hostile takeover in the mid 1990s.

Another industry that is often overlooked is malting. The process of malting converts raw grain into malt through forced germination. It produces malt suitable for brewing, distilling and a wide range of other uses. Since malting barley grows well in the Suffolk climate (in the pre-irrigation days it was one of the few crops which could be grown well on very light land), the industry has always been important locally. Maltings have been considered by some to be unattractive buildings: plain brick on the outside with gloomy interiors. However,

Snape Maltings was converted during the mid 1960s to become an internationally famous concert venue and burgeoning cultural and tourist centre. The success of the venture has helped to stimulate interest in old malt houses.

Until about 1860, almost all malting was carried out on a very small scale. As the nineteenth century grew older the large brick-built maltings, many of which are still a feature of the landscape, began to mushroom up all over East Anglia.

Practically all Suffolk towns had numerous maltings – Woodbridge is reputed to have had thirty. Most of them were small backyard operations which are untraceable, but there is no reason to doubt their existence, for many of them must have been 'one-man' maltings. It's likely they were part of an outbuilding of a large house, or behind an inn – a reminder of the days when every landlord brewed his own beer. There are still several of the steep, slate-roofed kilns to be seen around the town, but the largest were Waterloo Maltings (formerly Ingram Smith's builder's yard, now a luxury accommodation development) and Melton Hill Maltings (now the upmarket Deben Mills development with accommodation and a business centre).

Another industry that was naturally to be found in this great corn growing area was milling. The milling of wheat for flour is not a forgotten industry, but grinding it by wind and water power certainly is. The sails of a windmill turning slowly against the background of a vast blue sky was a common sight to former generations. When, in 1830, the journalist and anti-Corn Law campaigner, William Cobbett rode into Ipswich to collect impressions for his book 'Rural Rides', he counted no less than seventeen mills at work. He was delighted and, considering he was usually quick to point out faults, this was quite a compliment. From his enthusiastic description, we know the mills were painted white, or whitewashed, and the sails were black. This colour scheme seems to have been reversed later because most surviving mills, and those recalled in living memory, are black (originally tar) with white painted sails.

The sight of a windmill at work held a fascination for Edward

**Shottisham Watermill and the Mill House. 2017.**

FitzGerald. It seems there were three windmills standing on the hill behind Woodbridge in his day. Once, when one of these was under threat of being dismantled, he purchased a piece of land to prevent this happening. Keene wrote that this definitely made him one of the 'right sorts'. But, although FitzGerald saved one mill, he could not save them all. When large roller mills were established at the ports, where there was an unlimited supply of imported grain coming in, the slow, stone-grinding village mills were doomed.

Even in 1933, Suffolk had sixty-four mills working; twenty-nine were water-powered, and thirty-five relied on wind. Norfolk had sixty mills relying on wind and water power, and most other counties, far less. Woodbridge is lucky to have one of the few surviving windmills.

Woodbridge's surviving
windmill, Buttrum's Mill.

This is Buttrum's Mill, a tower style mill, built in 1836 and repaired in 1954 by the East Suffolk County Council and the Pilgrim Trust, at a cost of just under £4,000. There was also a move at one time to restore Tricker's Mill just off Theatre Street, but the owner of the coal business and the ground surrounding it did not want intruders in his yard. This tower mill stands on what was once Black Barn Farm, and John Tricker worked the mill until around 1920.

Like Tricker's Mill, Burgh Mill has also had its cap and sails removed. In this case the operation was carried out in 1934. Previously there was another mill, sited slightly to the east of the present Burgh Mill, and constructed of red bricks, some of which are now the Mill House garden wall. The last miller at Burgh is reputed to have kept his money under the floor and always wore a top hat when he went to market – as befitted a man of real substance.

One of the unusual facts about windmills is that they were sometimes dismantled and moved to a fresh site. Gedding Mill was moved twice; the last time in 1867 when it was moved from Felsham. Bedingfield's Mill came from Oakley and Tannington's Mill was first worked at Framlingham.

Using wooden rollers and twenty horses, Wingfield's post mill was dragged three miles from Syleham. This was in the late nineteenth century and a Mr Wingfield instigated the move. This family's connection with the village is a very long one. In 1361 Sir John Wingfield built Wingfield's church and a year later, the College of Wingfield. Part of the college still stands, although it was dissolved in 1542. In 1384, the Wingfield heiress, Katherine, was married to Michael de la Pole. It was this ambitious nobleman who became Earl of Suffolk and built Wingfield Castle, the remains of which are now a moated farmhouse that at one time had a drawbridge.

Even though the Wingfields lost their land, they remained in the village. The four grandsons of the man who moved the mill went on to farm the 300-acre Lodge Farm. Their grandfather had left the mill to an aunt and, in 1945, she sold it to an artist, Jack Penton. One of the Lodge Farm brothers, Ivor Wingfield, used to play around the mill as a schoolboy, and in 1967 he bought it back. It was his ambition

Webster's Mill, Framsden, 1965. Photograph: Wikimedia Commons user: Felix O

to restore the mill to working order but, unfortunately, in 1987, one of the front corner posts failed and the mill was blown down in a fierce gale.

A little nearer Framlingham is a very similar post mill at Framsden. Here Samuel Webster ground corn by 'wind and steam', the steam being the steam engine driving the mill when there was not enough wind. This was a common practice in the last days of windmills, but even then they could not compete with the Ipswich roller mills – as they could not produce white flour, they were forced to grind corn for cattle food. Also at Framsden, there is a Simper's Farm with Simper's Hill behind it, on the Tollemache estate.

My grandfather Herman Simper (1877–1961) was born at Framsden and toiled for many years growing wheat and beans in Charsfield. I remember he would always enquire whether any farm under discussion could grow good wheat. This was an old test of land – if it could not give a high yield of wheat, then it could not give a man a reasonable income. Suffolk farmers stuck with this theory for too long, although not much could have been done to prevent it.

During the 1920s and 30s, rural Suffolk had a pretty thin time. This was corn-growing land, yet many fields were derelict and overgrown, while Gustav Erikson's beautiful square-riggers brought Australian grain halfway round the world to Ipswich for less cost than it took to produce locally. The plight of the unemployed industrial worker and miner during the Depression is a theme that has been written about a great deal, but the sad case of 'over employment' in agriculture during these hard times is almost forgotten.

William Frederick Turner, my great grandfather, was not bound to any traditional outlook during this Depression. I can just remember him as a small, determined man who persuaded me, a small, stubborn boy, to go for a walk with him to look at some sugar beet one hot summer's evening.

William Turner left his home farm, which was near Nottingham, to seek his fortune in London. His mother sent him off with a bundle of home grown food. As he walked to the station, he amused himself by throwing hard-boiled eggs at the telegraph poles. In the years he spent in the East End of London, he was often hungry, and wished he had not wasted those eggs. By the time he arrived in Suffolk, he was a much wiser man, having built up a tailoring business, employing Russian Jews, before selling up and returning to his first love, the land.

He settled in Somerset for a while, but moved on to the eastern counties, where land was much cheaper. Every Tuesday, he went to Ipswich Market and often attended farm sales. Periodically, he bought farms he had neither seen nor knew where they were. He acquired farms all over the place, and would set likely young men up in business. All of this gave him a great deal of pleasure. But for all his enthusiasm, he never made a fortune. In fact, his only real achievement was not going 'bust' when his neighbours did.

When coming to Suffolk, he had not reckoned on the cost of labour necessary for arable farming. In the grasslands, he knew, labour was practically nil. Even though the workers' wages were then pretty grim, they were expensive to the landowner when his crops were practically being given away.

W.F. Turner is credited with having been the first man in the county to own a milking machine, which he installed on his farm near Needham Market. At one stage he lived at Home Farm, Capel St Andrew, and had the large, neighbouring, light-land farm rent-free for two years. This was quite a normal custom during those depressing years. Many landlords almost had to bribe tenants to stay in order to keep their land in cultivation. On a 2,000 acre estate at Stoke-by-Nayland, the rents were seven shillings and sixpence an acre, out of which the landlord had to pay six shillings and sixpence an acre for tithe. During the two years William Turner had his rent-free farm, the agents were trying to find a buyer as the previous owner had gone bankrupt. In the end, the agent offered the farm to him at four pounds an acre, which he quickly declined, pointing out that he could buy all the wheat-growing land he wanted for two pounds an acre. However, when the agent did find a buyer offering a better price, Turner wasted no time, and sold his farm as well. Real money was worth a thousand promises. After this, he gave up farming, having had a difficult but worthwhile life being his own boss.

While the Depression stunted all progress, windmills lingered on, as part of the country scene. It would have been a great pity if they had all been pulled down as soon as their usefulness was over. The author, Rex Wailes, described the East Suffolk post mills as the finest of their type, not only in England, but also in the world, and fortunately one of these has survived at Saxtead Green. The first mention of a windmill at Saxtead occurs in the Framlingham survey of 1309. Quite when the present mill was built is not known, but the records of one standing on this site go back to 1796. Robert Holmes built the mill house in 1810. The last miller to work it, a Mr A.S. Aldred, died in 1947.

During Mr Aldred's time, a steam traction engine was used to drive the mill when there was not enough wind. Often, during the winter, the traction engine was used out on the farm to drive the thrashing drums – 'throsh'en tackles' we used to call them – and after the farm men went home, it was returned to the mill to drive it all through the night. It came back to the farm again the next morning. Mr Aldred also owned a windmill at Worlingworth and, during the

Saxtead Green Post Mill. Photograph: Amanda Slater.

First World War, the mill's fantail was painted a patriotic red, white and blue. Saxtead Green Mill, however, has always been painted white and blue – and very attractive it looks. Actually, the old millers often referred to their mills as 'she', just like ships. Wind-driven mills and ships have many things in common; both require skilful handling to prevent them from being overpowered by this fierce element. The Saxtead Green Mill has since been overhauled and English Heritage opens it to the public.

Suffolk is a county of slow-running streams, but it was still possible to harness their flow to produce power. Water wheels were put to much wider usage than the region's windmills, which usually only ground corn or pumped water. The Old Paper Mill at Bramford, for instance, was worked as such from 1717 to 1793, and then, up to 1880, it was also used for corn milling. Glemsford Mill was built in 1825 as a silk-throwing mill. Hoxne Mill was used to produce textiles, flax and linen and to grind corn, before it closed in 1928.

It is thought that in the middle of the nineteenth century there were 27,000 watermills in the British Isles. As far as Suffolk is concerned, the sites of seventy-three watermills have been identified. Although this is a large cereal growing area and naturally a centre of the milling industry, once cheap imported grain began to arrive at the large ports, towards the end of the nineteenth century, watermills steadily declined in number. By 1968 the only remaining working mills were Baylham, Layham, Pakenham, Raydon and Wickham Market. There does not seem to have been any pattern of mill closure. Nothing dramatic happened, they just faded away.

The Bucklesham Mill does not appear to have been worked after 1930, and four years after this it was adapted as a pumping station to supply Felixstowe with water. Shottisham Mill, which in 1536 was the home of Bathelmew the miller, was worked up to 1952.

At the head of Butley Creek stands a water mill that has been owned by the Hewitt family for several generations. The original Butley Mill is thought to have been sited some two miles further inland, near Staverton Park, and to have been moved down in 1535. An undershot wheel drove the present mill; that is, the water passed under the bottom of the wheel. Rarely in East Anglia were there any overshot wheels with water coming from on top, because of the lack of fall. At one stage, a windmill stood on the high ground just behind Butley Mill. After this was pulled down, horses were used to drag a replacement mill from Martlesham but this one was destroyed by fire, a common fate for windmills because of friction on the wooden mechanism. Following this, in about 1890, it was replaced with a roller mill beside the watermill. Further down, on the opposite side of the creek, there once stood a wind-driven drainage pump.

Mr Hewitt tells me that before the First World War, barges came right up Butley Creek to a jetty 500 yards below the mill. The *Eaglet*, owned by Ipswich millers R. & W. Paul, used to bring maize regularly. Mr Hewitt's father grew lupins that thrived on the light land and his enterprise earned him the title of the 'Lupin King'. The lupins were shipped to Belgium to be used for dye making. Much of Butley Creek is now grown up with reeds used for thatching.

The waters of the River Deben drove six mills at one time, and the tidal waters at Woodbridge drove another one. The Deben's source is near the village of Debenham, and the first mill placed along the downstream route was at the small, heavy-land village of Kettleburgh. Kettleburgh mill had three 'stones', but there often wasn't enough water to drive them. In about 1873, a smock mill was moved from Tuddenham, and when the miller was short of water, he could use this windmill. However, there must have been periods during the summer months when both mills were stopped. When Kettleburgh Mill was dismantled, the wheel was taken to Shottisham Mill and used as an overshot wheel, but most of the smock mill parts were taken to Parham Post Mill.

From Letheringham, the Deben winds its way down between the water meadows to Deben Mill at Wickham Market. The deeds of this building go back to 1701, but it is quite possibly older. Robert Martin, the Beccles millwright who looked after this mill for many years, always maintained that the water wheel was of a type usually made long before the earliest deed date. This wheel weighs twelve and a half tons and has a diameter of sixteen feet. When I visited it in 1968, it was still being worked daily and so, too, was the iron pit wheel which was installed in 1880. This is typical of the slow-moving gears of a mill; they seem to have rumbled on for decades, requiring little attention.

The Deben Mill had sufficient water to be worked for twenty-four hours a day, except perhaps during a very dry summer. However, it was once run in conjunction with a four, common-sailed windmill. This mill was pulled down in 1868 and the bricks were used to build a steam mill. In 1885, the milling business was taken over by Ruben

Rackham and he put up the Deben roller mill, about forty yards east of the watermill, to take the record harvest of 1893.

The steel-roller method of milling wheat was perfected in central Europe in the 1860s. Later, when introduced into England, the traditional stone-grinding system was doomed to extinction. It is an odd twist of fate that the Deben roller mill ceased to work first, in 1949, while the watermill continued in use.

The Deben roller mill, amongst others, was driven by a steam engine manufactured by Whitmore & Binyon, a local firm which had its head office at 64 Mark Lane, London. The machines all proudly bore the address of their works at 'Wickham Market, England'. The engine that went into the mill was twenty-five feet long with a nine and a half foot flywheel. Since being taken out, its owners have very kindly presented it to the East Anglian Museum of Rural Life at Stowmarket.

The milling business was operated by E.R. & R.T. Rackham Ltd whose activities were not wholly confined to grinding corn. The watermill was still worked because of the interest taken in it by Ruben Rackham's two sons, Edward and Robert Rackham. Edward Rackham began work at the Deben mill in 1910 and, as the only man left with the necessary knowledge, he worked the water mill until his death in 1970. The flour ground there was sold to local bakeries. Although the mill had three stones, each 'stone' weighing eight hundredweight (8cwt = $8 \times 112$lbs), only two stones were worked at once. Edward Rackham was told the three stones used to be worked all at once, but this was never done during his time. He believed it would throw too much strain on the great crown wheel. The massive wheel had 120 wooden cogs, which were renewed in 1927. Mr Rackham lived in the house on the end of the mill and, as a consequence, avoided introducing iron cogs because they would have made too much noise.

A little further downstream is another mill rented by Ruben Rackham and, later, the Rackham brothers worked it for three days a week. The owners, Loudham Estate, worked it for the other three. Edward Rackham always knew it as Ash Mill, and worked it until its preservation in 1956. He would work the Wickham Market mill in the morning, and then, in the afternoon cycle down to Ash Mill and use the same water to grind there. The mill never used any other power except water. Unusually, it could be driven with only two foot of water at the sluice gates.

The millers probably used the name Ash Mill because it was simple to say, but it was also referred to as Campsea Ashe Mill, Ashe Abbey Mill, and more recently, Loudham Mill. The original mill was built by the Augustinian Canons of Campsea Ashe Abbey, which was founded before 1195. The remains of this priory are near Abbey Farm House and here, in 1843, six stone coffins were dug up.

The remaining two mills that stood on the Deben have both been turned into attractive houses. Both were quite small mills. The one at Ufford ceased to work in 1916, and the last miller from Melton Mill moved to Ipswich in about 1896.

The Tide Mill at Woodbridge is one of the most unusual industrial buildings in Britain. It has had a long and useful career spanning nine centuries and must have provided flour for many generations of people living in the town. The first mention of the Tide Mill was in 1170 when the canons of Woodbridge Priory granted Baldwin de Ufford a plot of land so he could have easy access to the mill. These early records do not state the type of mill but, since no possible alternative site has been found for de Ufford's mill, it is assumed that it stood in its present position. This is the first known record of a tide mill in the British Isles.

Before reclamation, the Deben reached further inland and it is possible Station Road was, originally, just above the high tide mark. Presumably, a medieval quay reached from the Boat Inn to the Tide Mill. At that time, a small stream, starting in the grounds of Woodbridge School, flowed down across the Thoroughfare, down Brook Street and ran out into the Deben on the southern side of the Tide Mill. In eighteenth century prints, the course of this stream can still be seen coming out near the mill. The stream is now piped, but before this it could have washed away silt and kept the berths open. The present Ferry Dock must have been developed to provide suitable places to discharge cargo as ships grew larger.

The mill was an important part of the local economy and, in 1436,

Sir Robert Willoughby granted it to the Priory. At the dissolution of the monasteries it returned to the ownership of the Crown and, in 1564, Elizabeth I granted it to Thomas Seckford. It is thought to have remained in Seckford's possession until 1672.

No evidence has yet been discovered to decide accurately when the present four-storey structure was built. The most likely period is in the second half of the seventeenth century. At this time, shipbuilding for the Royal Navy was flourishing in the town.

The workings of Woodbridge mill are like an ordinary watermill. The difference lies purely in that tidal water would be trapped in the pond on the incoming tide and used to drive the mill during the following ebb tide. Some tide mills had ponds that were also fed by fresh water but, at Woodbridge, the mill relied solely on its seven and a half acre pond of salt water. The work done in the Tide Mill was, of course, tidal, and once the flood tide had covered the ferry hard there was insufficient fall of water to turn the wheel. Although there is said to have been enough power to drive all four of the mill's stones at once, only three ever worked together during the last years of its commercial milling life before 1957. At this point, the Tide Mill was closed for over a decade until the first of two major restoration projects was launched in 1968, when the building began its journey towards becoming an operational heritage site or living museum.

In a map of 'Town and Port of Woodbridge' drawn by Isaac Johnson in 1827, the mill and its granary appear to be just as they have survived until recent years. A little later, the premises were owned by George Manby and worked by John Benn. The machinery was then valued at £258 and the tenant's fixtures at £41. In the 1830s, ownership of the Tide Mill passed to the Hayward family who were the in-laws of John Manby.

A photograph taken in the 1860s shows a white, weather-boarded Tide Mill and granary and, alongside the quay, two tops'l schooners are discharging. A. Hayward & Son traded as corn merchants from here. By the turn of the century, the Haywards had clad the mill's distinctive weatherboarding in ugly corrugated iron sheeting. While it didn't look picture perfect, the cladding did serve to preserve the

The crew of the barge *Freston Tower* sweeping the deck while the 'humpers' watch on Tide Mill Quay.

skin of the mill and strengthen its structure. Also, by this time, business expediency saw a progression from grinding only local grown corn towards bringing in cheaper, imported wheat. The Haywards expanded the business by building a steam mill opposite the gas works, where there was a reliable supply of water.

At the time, regular barge traffic brought in wheat, although after the nineteenth century the flour was not taken away by water. As a young man, Arthur Thorpe unloaded barges at the Tide Mill Quay. At Woodbridge 'dockers' were known as 'humpers' and were employed on a daily basis. Arthur recalled that it took a gang of six men to unload a barge. The operation was carried out by hand: two men down in the barge's hold, two men on the winch lifting the sacks to deck level, and two men carrying sacks on their backs up a plank to the second storey of the granary. They reckoned to unload a barge in a day and a half. Chubb Horlock came here with wheat in the Mistley barge *Memory* in about 1913. He worked the hand winch lifting the heavy coomb sacks out of the hold and remembered it was very hard work for a fourteen-year old boy. It is doubtful if any wheat was brought in by water after 1926.

In about 1932, the Tide Mill wheel, installed by Collins of Melton some 80 years previously, began to give trouble. Amos Clark was commissioned to build a new wheel on the old shaft. This millwright was closely connected with the mill during the last years it was in full operation.

Amos Clark was born in 1875 at Weybread and his family owned land at Debenham. He learnt the trade of a millwright from his father, the secrets of this craft having been handed down successively from his great-grandfather. As a young man, he worked in London, but during the First World War, he brought his family back to Suffolk. He established himself at Woodbridge and looked after Tricker's, Buttrum's and the Tide Mill. Mills seldom had names but were often known by the men who worked them. Just at the end of the war, he moved to Charsfield and then to Parham. Here, he had the black-smith's shop and also owned the Mendlesham Post Mill, which was worked by his brother, George. Next, Amos Clark moved to Grundis-burgh, and while he was there, he pulled down Mr Nunn's Mill.

After the war, there was a great shortage of seasoned oak, which was in demand to be used as facing on mock Tudor houses. Amos employed up to eight men and, during the following two decades, he and his posse pulled down over eighty wind and watermills in the Eastern Counties. This must have been a sad task for a man whose real vocation was to repair them. It was a job that could only be done once and fortunately, not everyone wanted the mill destroyed. Amar's knowledge was in very great demand by the time of the Second World War as there were, by then, few craftsmen able to look after the remaining mills that used stones for grinding.

Apart from the Tide Mill wheel, another of his accomplishments was the construction of a huge pit-wheel for the Duke of Grafton's Sapson watermill in Buckinghamshire. This was in about 1942, by which time Amos had settled at Belle Vue Road, Ipswich. He built the Sapson wheel in his tiny back garden and the neighbours were most intrigued to see Amos's handmade masterpiece take shape. At the time, though, his family was not impressed. The operation ruined the garden and caused quite an upheaval when the wheel had to be taken apart in sections and carried through to the road to be loaded on the lorry.

In 1950, he repaired the famous Pakenham Mill near Bury St Edmunds. This fine tower mill had been damaged in a gale two years previously and Amos restored it to working order with full sails. He continued as a millwright up to the end of his seventy-eight years. All his four sons were apprenticed to his craft, but later went into other occupations. The last to carry on the family tradition was his younger brother, George Clark. The two brothers had worked together for many years. During the 1930s, they had moved an attractive post mill from Aldringham to Thorpeness, where it was used as a water pump at the seaside holiday village. The Aldringham miller hated to see his beloved mill being dismantled, so the Clarks used to work on it when he was at Chapel, on Sundays. When they re-erected it, they put a half crown under the post for luck.

Until the Second World War there was nothing unique about the Woodbridge Tide Mill – it was part of everyday life – but after the war it became obvious it would be the last survivor of its kind. A 1938 survey, finished by Rex Wailes, revealed that there were then twenty-three tide mills left in Britain, of which only nine were still being worked by water. There had been tide mills at Dunwich and Ipswich, both of which had long since stopped. The Walton-on-the-Naze mill was pulled down in 1921 and the post mill beside it collapsed the day the demolition of the tide mill was completed.

A better-known Essex tide mill stood at Saint Osyth and worked until 1930. In 1962, after being derelict for years, it was blown down. Another, at Fingringhoe, straddles the creek. Additional milling buildings have been added so it remains useful, although it ceased to function a long time ago. Maldon seems to have had one at Mill Beach, but all traces have gone.

I believe that one of the Cornish tide mills ran until a little after the Second World War. Its closure left Woodbridge as the only one working in the British Isles and the whole circumference of the North Sea. In 1950, a preservation scheme costing £500 was carried out with the support of, among others, the Suffolk Preservation Society. Again, the wheel began to give trouble; the original shaft was by then over a hundred years old. In the following summer, the wedges that secured the wheel fell out and floated away on the tide, leaving the wheel thrashing around in a drunken fashion until it was stopped. More frequent causes of damage were through children throwing wood into the millpond. Some of this driftwood got through the sluice and knocked the paddles off the apple-wood wheel. This meant Jack Hawes had to drive into Ipswich to collect Amos Clark to put the damage right.

In 1954 the Witnesham farmer John Matthews, bought A. Hayward & Son. He modernised the plant and installed a diesel engine in the Tide Mill. It was no longer viable to use water power alone, as grinding could only take place a few hours each side of low water and this meant working at least one night shift. The time had come when on a cold winter's night while the wind screamed around the old, time-worn mill, a dusty miller was no longer required to tend the gently rumbling mill by the soft light of an oil lamp. The tide that came creeping over the mud and lapped round the footings twice a day went unheeded. So, by 1957 it was all finished. Or so it was thought. The town of Woodbridge wanted the buildings to be pulled down.

Luckily a saviour, in the form of Mrs Jean Gardner from Wickham-brook, arrived just as the mill was about to be lost forever. Her husband asked her over breakfast what she would like for her birthday and she said 'Woodbridge Tide Mill'. This was 1968, the Tide Mill had stood idle for a decade and Claude Whisstock, from Whisstocks Boatyard, had purchased the pond that had provided the power to drive the mill wheel. He wanted to turn it into a yacht harbour and intend-ed to acquire the Tide Mill in order to demolish it and increase his development space. Because the mill was in such poor condition, most people in Woodbridge agreed that it should be pulled down. The ruined mill sold for the price of a good house in the town and then, aided by her husband Rodney, Mrs Gardner set up a charitable trust and a local support group, and a programme of repairs was set in motion.

The building was given a thorough overhaul; foundations were shored up, it received replacement pantiles on the roof, the corrugated steel cladding was removed and the original weatherboarding brought back to life. The machinery was overhauled and perhaps most significantly, in 1976, the waterwheel was replaced, thanks to the skill of millwright Derek Ogden. The programme took several years to complete, but in 1972 the Woodbridge Tide Mill once more opened its doors, to a warm fanfare from the local community and heritage enthusiasts who came to visit.

However, no matter how much love and attention the Tide Mill received, the old building needed continual nurturing. The sale of the millpond had left the new wheel without the natural power to drive it. In order to keep it evenly moist and preserve its lifespan, Peter Wyllie would regularly walk around the wheel keeping it wet. Thus, when in 1981 Lord Cranbrook donated a quantity of mud and clay to construct the walls of a new tide pool it was named Wyllie's Pool in recognition of his loyal efforts.

Fishing and shell fishing were never a large industry in the Deben, but they were always there. Before World War I the Woodbridge pilots went fishing when there were no barges around. They had small clinker smacks for trawling for flat fish; the last of these was the *Jem Mace*. Eels could be caught in the eelgrass upriver from Tide Mill, for these they had open rowing boats with wet wells in order to store them alive. They also rowed right down to the reach above Felixstowe Ferry and set Peter nets on posts at low water, before rowing back on the flood tide.

In contrast to the flat fish and eels, the shellfish were all lower down the river. Before World War I, 'Kio' Collins used to go winkling on the low tide line at Ramsholt, collecting winkles to take on his

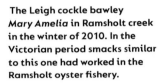

The Leigh cockle bawley
*Mary Amelia* in Ramsholt creek
in the winter of 2010. In the
Victorian period smacks similar
to this one had worked in the
Ramsholt oyster fishery.

donkey around the villages for sale. As a prank the schoolboys from
Alderton used to throw water on the slope on the Alderton Road so
in a hard frost the donkey slipped over. In the 1930s Ruben Mann
of Shottisham kept a boat at Stonner Point and was known as the
'Great British Winkler,' as he also traded winkles in the surrounding
villages. Though the winkles and eelgrass vanished in the late 1930s,
there was still eel fishing in the ditches and mullet fishing in the river
until the 1980s.

In the 1930s three unemployed men joined together to harvest
and sell the mussels from Waldringfield beach. Ray Lord remembered
seeing these men and was inspired to restart mussel farming forty
years later, first in the Stonner Channel and then moving them all up
river to Methersgate Reach.

In about 1965 the Bawdsey Fleet was deepened and a large number of old oyster shells came out, which turned out to be the remains of a medieval oyster fishery. When the fresh water Shottisham Creek was deepened in 1977 likewise a lot of native oyster shells came out. This must have been from the oyster beds run in 1796 by Thomas Abbott of Ramsholt. He built his own smacks, but unfortunately went out of business which led to the creek being dammed off for cattle grazing. In 1885, Charles Barras, a London gentleman and yacht owner, started the Ramsholt oyster fishery with storage pits near Green Point. Barras brought in crews on West Mersea smacks to work the oyster beds, but in 1891 he sold out to the Government's United Oyster Company. The fishery eventually petered out, leaving only the native oysters in the river.

In the 1980s Waldringfield Harbour Master started oyster cultivation with quick growing pacific oysters, which were left to grow wild in the river when he ceased farming. In 2011 my grandson Harry Simper wanted to work on the river so he searched in the boat *Pet* at low tide and found the places where oysters and mussels were growing wild. We then rented Hemley Creek from the Crown Estates and started cultivation of Pacific oysters. The Deben water is second cleanest in England where there are shellfish. We have used several boats in this fishery; mostly open outboard boats: *Little Pearl*, named after son Jonathan and Clare's daughter Sara Pearl, and *Little Princess* named after our great-granddaughter Hollie. In the Woodbridge area mussels are in far more demand than oysters, although Simper's Silver Harvest still continues to sell them. Jonathan's 1914 Leigh cocker *Mary Amelia* is sometimes still used to move large loads of mussels around.

# SIX

# Ships and Shipping

The Romans must have considered the River Deben an important port because they built a fort to protect against attack from Saxon pirates. This fort was Portus Adurni and it stood on the cliffs overlooking the Deben entrance. It was one of a series of forts built on the coast from Porchester to Brancaster, completed before the year 337 under the command of the Count of the Saxon Shore. A small fleet of ships which attacked raiding Saxons was connected to these forts and would probably have been based in King's Fleet, Falkenham.

Portus Adurni was abandoned when the Romans retreated to mainland Europe and it fell into disrepair. The ruins were rebuilt as Walton Castle in the medieval period and the first definite record of it was in 1101 when Henry I granted Framlingham Castle to Roger Bigod, and Walton Castle became part of his land.

Although it withstood several armed attacks, it couldn't keep the sea back. Every storm nibbled away at the sandy coast and took more land so that eventually Walton Castle fell into the sea. Most Suffolk coastal villages have at least one village, sometimes several villages, out on the seabed in front of them. In 1722 sheep were still grazing around the ruins of Walton Castle, but not long afterwards the cliff collapsed into the sea. On a very low spring tide the remains of Walton Castle come to surface just in front of the Dip at Old Felixstowe. These ruins are believed to have been the inner gatehouse.

There were cliffs on either side of the entrance to the Deben and about two kilometres appear to have been lost to the sea on the Felixstowe and Bawdsey sides since the medieval period. The wide river mouth at Harwich was difficult to defend but the narrow entrance of the Deben at Bawdsey meant the river could be defended against attacking pirates. This might have encouraged the Anglo-Saxon dynasty of the Wufflings to make their base at the head of the Deben. However the narrow, difficult entrance didn't prevent the French from creeping in and burning the king's ships that were lying at anchor in the King's Fleet in the medieval period.

During this period there were two great fleets on either side of river mouth ('fleet' was an East Coast word for a shallow creek, cutting into the countryside). On the Felixstowe shore, King's Fleet ran up to Walton Manor, and Bawdsey Fleet was on the other side nearly up to Alderton. The king held Walton Manor and used the King's Fleet to assemble warships for the endless wars in Flanders (modern Belgium) whilst, across the water, enterprising merchants operated from the Bawdsey side. These two fleets and villages around them were collectively known as Gosford, although there doesn't appear to have ever been a single settlement of this name.

The early trade in the Sandlings villages originally went through Gosford, but the fleets slowly silted up, a natural process that still goes on today. Reeds grew where ships had once ridden at anchor and there was barely enough water for swans to swim. Once the channels became too shallow for shipping, they were walled off for valuable summer grazing for cattle and horses. As sheep can survive without water for several days, they remained up on the heathlands. By the 1600s the trade had moved inland to Woodbridge, and Gosford had disappeared. Even the entrance of the river had changed its name to Woodbridge Haven.

Woodbridge had its share of the lucrative wool trade and the industrious Tudor merchants expanded the port. The first customs house was erected on Woodbridge Quay in 1589, but sometime at the latter end of the following century it was moved to Quay Street. By then, the port was thriving and the annual revenue on Suffolk cloth alone amounted to £2,722.

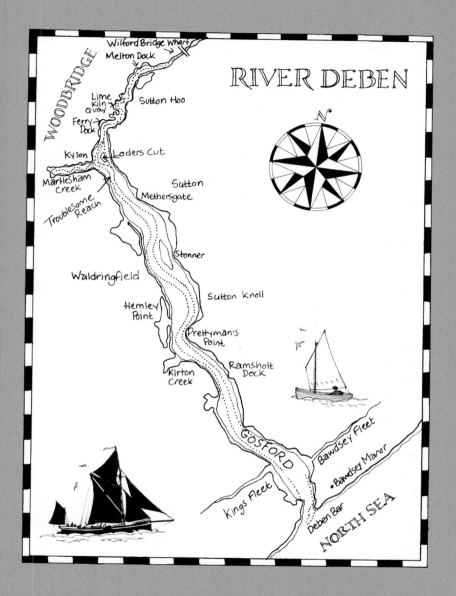

Although there was a plentiful supply of oak near Woodbridge, the lack of water must have made it difficult to launch a large ship here. Harwich and Ipswich began to take the lead but, Woodbridge was approaching its golden age as a shipbuilding centre in the 16th and early 17th century. Most of these vessels seem to have been built of Suffolk timber for London merchants. These included the 120 ton *Bark Smith* in 1566 and, in 1638, the 290 ton *Ann Francis* was launched into the Deben. Between 1625–1638 eleven large ships, including *Levant Merchant*, the *Muscovy Merchant*, both of 400 tons, and the 700 ton *Goodman* were built and launched at Woodbridge.

So Woodbridge was established as a shipbuilding centre, but timber was still being sold to the Royal Dockyard at Deptford on the Thames.

The great art of wooden shipbuilding was to choose the right trees with good timber, preferably selecting the trees whilst they were still standing. Phineas Pett was the master shipwright at Deptford and he used to visit Woodbridge for his timber-buying expeditions. Pett had built the fifty-five gun *Prince Royal* and, between 1635–37, the famous *Sovereign of the Seas*. These were then the finest warships afloat anywhere in the world and no doubt a great deal of Suffolk timber went into them. It took considerable effort and expense to ship the ungainly logs from the Deben to Deptford, so Pett decided that, since merchant ships were being built at Woodbridge and the town had many good shipwrights, it made sense to use Suffolk oak to build warships in the town. Once the Petts gave their support, things expanded rapidly.

Whilst in Woodbridge, Pett lodged at Thomas Cole's Crown Inn at the top of Quay Street. He eventually arranged for his fifth son, Peter Pett (1610–72) to marry Cole's daughter. The marriage took place in 1633 and, through his wife, Peter Pett gained property in Woodbridge that included the Crown Inn and Lime Kiln Dock.

The Lime Kiln Shipyard was the best place in Woodbridge to build ships. It was on a bend in the river where the deep water came close to the bank and a ship could be safely launched. The shipyard itself extended up to the Thoroughfare and the top end was used for timber storage. The large ships were built on a slipway that appears to have been roughly where the present Sun Wharf railway crossing is.

The *Prosperous Mary*, built in about 1635, was taken to Deptford to be rigged out. She came back later to load 171 tons of provisions at the town quay in Woodbridge to be delivered to the army in Scotland. Peter Pett became Master Shipwright at Chatham, and later, when as Navy Commissioner he was allowed to give contracts for the building of men-of-war, he saw to it that some of these went to Woodbridge. Thomas Adams, Edmund Munday and William Carey were given much sought-after contracts.

Peter Pett ran into deep political troubles though. He was following the custom of the day by giving lucrative state positions to his relations. His enemies would, no doubt, have done the same, but in the end they had him thrown out of office. Despite Pett's dismissal, the building of warships continued.

In 1675, the largest warship ever built on the Deben was launched into the Ferry Dock. This was Edmund Munday's 663 ton fourth-rater *Kingfisher*. The length of her gun deck was 125ft. This warship took part in the capture of Gibraltar but ended her career as a hulk in Harwich. The last warships from the town's yards, built in the closing years of the century, were the fifth-raters *Hastings* and *Ludlow*, both 381 tons with thirty-two guns. There was a description of Woodbridge in the *Suffolk Traveller*, written about thirty years later:

> Here are two Quays, the Common Quay where the chief Imports and Exports are, and where the fine "Woodbridge" salt is made, and above this is the Lime-kiln Quay where formerly the Ludlow Man of War was built. Some years hence another Dock below the Common Quay, where the Kingfisher Man of War was built, but this is now (cut) from the River by a mud Wall and almost filled up.

The first ships built for the navy were the fourth-rater *Advice*, which at 544 tons carried 230 men and forty-eight guns, and the 513-tonner *Reserve*, built in Woodbridge in 1650 at a cost of six pounds and ten shillings per ton. The practice was that, following the launch (the *Reserve* drew fifteen foot of water), the vessels were towed or sailed under jury rig (a basic rig with makeshift sails) to the Thames to be rigged out. The builder appears to have been under contract to supply the ships partially manned, but local men were not keen on the navy and preferred to serve at the Ipswich colliers where, even if the pay was bad, at least they received it.

Adams had trouble finding enough workmen to finish the frigate *Maidstone* and when she was completed he had to take command of her. The Dutch were then doing all they could to stop our coastal shipping and often large fleets of merchantmen lay in Harwich harbour. The *Maidstone* was employed to guard the coast after a Dutch frigate had chased a hoy (passenger carrying vessel) into Woodbridge Haven.

The Dutch wars caused a great demand for naval vessels and Woodbridge bore much of the burden during England's struggle for maritime supremacy over its rivals. Edmund Munday travelled to Woolwich to try and obtain the money owed for some timber he had sent. In 1653, General Blake landed 300 sick men, with orders for them to be cared for by the people of Woodbridge. Higher taxes were slapped on the townsfolk to raise the money needed to support the men. Many of Munday's and Carey's shipwrights promptly fled from the district. The town already had Dutch prisoners on its hands and it had also incurred heavy losses in a lawsuit against the Seckford family over the alms houses and trust money, all of which contributed to Woodbridge being in debt to the tune of £500.

While Oliver Cromwell remained Lord Protector, much attention was paid to the strength and general efficiency of the navy. In 1654, the 516 ton fourth-rater *Preston* was launched at Woodbridge, just a year after *Maidstone*. With the restoration of the monarchy in 1660 many ships were renamed; *Maidstone* became *Mary Rose* and was finally captured by the French in 1691. The *Preston* became the *Antelope* and was sold in 1693.

Woodbridge ships served the navy well, although at times it appears that their masters used them as privateers rather than for the high-minded ideal of instruments for national security. Only Edward Russell, who at one time was master of *Reserve*, rose to a high rank.

This colourful admiral destroyed the French fleet at La Hogue, and this won him the title Earl of Orford.

In 1660, on the announcement that Charles II was to be made king, the bells were rung in Saint Mary's church, Woodbridge. One man, however, still spoke well of the protectorate and was promptly taken before the magistrate and ordered to keep good behaviour.

At the time of the Restoration, steps were taken to make the measurement of ships more accurate. Since Elizabethan times, general confusion had grown up around the method of classifying ships by their tonnage. In theory, the term 'tons burthen' (tons burden) described the amount of cargo a vessel could carry. But cargo capacity was usually overestimated and ships carried less cargo than the number of tons they measured. The reformed system of 1660 attempted to address this, but still only gave a rough estimate. Therefore, Woodbridge-built ships such as the 350 ton *Darling* of London, the 300 ton *Resolution* of Aldeburgh and the 200 ton *Protection* of Ipswich were, in fact, a good deal smaller than their tonnage suggests. Another case is the *Goodman*, built in 1634 and described as being 700 tons, but she would not have been nearly the same size as a modern coaster of that description.

There was no lack of work for the town's shipwrights. From 1630 to the end of the century, fifteen men-of-war were launched here, and repair work was also done. While *Centurion* was being repaired in 1658, her bowsprit broke and six men were drowned. In 1666, when the plague swept through the town, killing over 300 people, the frigate *Albermarle* was launched.

It must have been a difficult time to complete a wooden ship. The labour requirements were enormous; every piece of wood had to be sawn by hand. One man stood on top of the sawpit and another below and both worked the saw up and down – hard, thirsty work. For this reason, trees seldom reached their maturity and were felled when quite young so that they could be transported and sawn up easily.

In the eighteenth century Woodbridge remained a port and shipbuilding centre, but few records of that time have survived. The only shipyard at this time was the Lime Kiln Yard. The actual lime kilns stood on the ground between the Gladwell Dock and Sun Wharf. This area's connection with the timber trade lasted until the 1920s, as little Scandinavian square-riggers used to bring cargoes to Messrs Brown's Yard, which then occupied what is now the downriver end of Robertsons Boatyard. Like all the deep-draught vessels that visited Woodbridge, the Norwegian brigantines had to discharge part of their cargoes into two lighters (barges that took some of the burden) at Kyson Point. This reduced the ships' draught and enabled them to move upriver and continue discharging their cargo.

Shipbuilding has always been a precarious occupation. In 1751, Edward Darley went bankrupt despite owning both the Boat Inn and the Anchor Inn. The timber merchant Samuel Turner took over, and built ships. In 1764, he built a ship for the Jamaica trade capable of transporting 240 tonnes at a time (the measurement known as burden tonne, to measure the amount the ship could carry). This was the largest to have been built in the town after the men-of-war, but the capital outlay must have been too much for Turner. Perhaps the buyers did not honour their agreement; bad debts can ruin any organisation. Whatever the cause, Turner went bankrupt not long after the ship had left the Deben.

The next builder of note was William Dryden who came to Lime Kiln in 1796 and produced a number of vessels for the coastal trade. Some of his larger vessels were the 150 ton brig *Britannia* and the packet *Henry Freeling* (under Captain P.C. Mason) which was used on the Harwich to Holland passenger and mail services. Some of the brigs could only carry 100 tons of cargo but, for all the dangers in their trade, they must have paid their way quite quickly. The 180 ton brig *Union*, built in 1815, went back to the Lime Kiln Yard for a major rebuild sixteen years later.

In 1818 Dryden sold the yard because his health had given out, though his retirement was short as he died in the following year. The yard was taken over by William Bayley who, before the end of the year, had launched a 'fine cutter' and a brig, with only a week between them. In 1820, he performed the unusual feat of launching the schooner *Commerce* fully rigged.

Two trading sloops at Tide Mill Quay in about 1830 with a capstan out on a shoal to haul them out. Image courtesy of Christian Knight.

About this time, William Garrard re-established the yard at the Common Quay. This area is now known as the Ferry Dock, and even then, Garrard's was sometimes referred to as the Dock Yard. He was responsible for the schooner *Mary & Betsy*, the sloops *Sarah*, *Hope* and *Lark* and a six-oar galley 'for gentlemen to row'. Later, William Garrard & Son of Brook Street operated as boatbuilders and shipowners with controlling shares in the sloop *Sportsman* until she was sold to the banker Frederick Alexander. At one stage, they were also outright owners of the *Hebe*.

Bayley seems to have expanded the Lime Kiln's capacity, but not everything was a complete success. He attempted to launch the *Bessie*

Previous pages: A collier brig being discharged of coal in Ferry Dock, Woodbridge in about 1850. When the East Suffolk Railway Line was constructed the dock in the foreground was filled in. One of the Woodbridge lighters can be seen along side the brig while the warehouses on the left appear to have been pulled down in the 1890s. Painted by James George Rowe.

with 150 people standing on deck. The schooner fell over on the slip, but was 'saved' and later successfully floated into the Deben. When the *Fame* was launched in 1824, Bayley had three other schooners on the yard in various stages of completion. One of the schooners was for Mr J. Cobbold. Unfortunately, Lime Kiln Yard did not offer enough scope for the ambitious Mr Bayley and he moved to Ipswich where he was, undoubtedly, one of the few to make a modest fortune in his calling.

Dryden's son, W. H. Dryden, took over Lime Kiln next, in 1826. The same year saw the launching of the 120 ton *Elizabeth*, which must have been the last brig completed there. Another of W. H. Dryden's vessels was the curiously named schooner, *Countess of Corker*. He also built the sloop *Mary Anne* which was christened by a small girl of the same name, but after only three years the yard was put up to let again.

William Taylor took over in 1830, and his shipwrights continued to meet the demand for coastal tonnage, with a long stream of tubby little schooners. Not all of them were for owners in the town. Southwold interests acquired *Albion*, and *Grecian Daughter* went to Manningtree. The keel was laid for another schooner for the same owners on the same day she was launched. Shipbuilding was then thriving, in an uncertain way.

In the first half of the nineteenth century the two-masted tops'l schooner was the most common rig used for trading vessels on the Suffolk coast. The single-masted vessels were sloops – rigs that are now known as gaff cutters. During this time, there was an average of about thirty schooners owned in, and fairly frequently trading to, Woodbridge. Certainly, they were not clippers, but round-bowed,

The Sea Scouts headquarters in Tide Mill Way is the former port of Woodbridge's Bond warehouse where expensive goods were stored.

with a pronounced tumblehome (narrowing beam, above the water-line) and square stern. Their appearance was solid and plain. They had no figureheads and the only decoration was the name, in white letters on the bow. Their purpose was to make a profit for their numerous shareholders and their voyages took them wherever profitable cargo-carrying work was available in European waters.

In one January gale, the sloop *Cumberland* was driven ashore at Southend, the schooner *Mary & Betsy* put into Ramsgate with her bulwarks (sides above deck level) washed away, and the *Hebe* was caught by the gale in the Sound between Denmark and Sweden. Both of *Hebe's* anchor cables parted and the schooner would have been driven ashore but a boat from HMS *Thunderer* reached her in time with another anchor and cable. Not all hazards were caused by the weather, though. In 1842, three schooners at the Common Quay were broken into. A gallon of whisky was lost from the *Thetis*, and the entire stock for a forthcoming voyage was stolen from the Yorkshire-built *Bee*.

The Woodbridge tops'l schooner *Bernard Barton* with a block rigged between the masts for hauling coal in baskets out of the vessel at the Ferry Quay coal yard. The *Bernard Barton* was the most famous of the Woodbridge schooners and sailed for nearly sixty years.

The best known Woodbridge schooner was the *Bernard Barton*. Her modest claim to fame does not entirely rest on the fact that she was named after the well-known poet, for this stout vessel appears to have outlasted her contemporaries. Before her launch on 21st April 1840, at least twenty-three other schooners had been completed at Lime Kiln Yard in the forty years prior, and nine followed her in the next few years. The *Bernard Barton* was registered as an 82 ton schooner, but sailors would have called her a tops'l schooner as she had two square sails on her foremast. Originally steered by a long tiller, she was typical of the little ships then being built.

A vessel is traditionally divided into sixty-four shares and the share ownership of the *Bernard Barton* was divided as follows: twenty-four shares were held by William Trott, sixteen by Cutting, while a miller and a farmer from Sutton each held eight and the remaining eight were held by the ship's master, Edward Passiful. Her voyages appear to have been between Liverpool and her home port. Presumably, the schooner's main function was to bring the animal feed, oil cake, round from Liverpool in the days before the railways came into being. Just after the railway finally reached Woodbridge, the *Bernard Barton* was laid up at Lime Kiln Quay with her sails taken off her spars.

The last schooner built at Woodbridge was the *Ellen*, built in 1853, and she sank off Yarmouth twenty-two years later. The *Gleaner* was broken up and the *Thomas* was cut down to become a lighter. At the same time the Sunderland-built *Sylph* was hulked, while the *Kate* sank in the North Sea. But some schooners were sold to fresh ports and eked out a living for a few more years. The *Friendship* went to Colchester, the *Brothers Friends* to South Shields and the *Bernard Barton* was sold to the West Country.

In 1851, William Trott had paid £120 at an auction for a fourth share in the *Bernard Barton*. He received a good deal less when she was sold. In 1862, the old schooner was taken to Poole and lengthened. The usual method was to saw the vessel in half and add some to the middle. After this, she became a ketch and was registered in Gloucester. In 1893 she was owned by Thomas Riddler and presumably worked to Porlock and Minehead. She finally sank off Lundy Island in 1899 while bound to Cardiff from Chichester with a cargo of wheat. A painting of the *Bernard Barton* in her glory days hangs in the Shire Hall, Woodbridge.

Going to sea was one of the ways a man could better himself in those far off days. The way was open for any capable young man to rise to command a schooner. Most of the masters also held a few shares in their vessels and in many cases, they eventually became shipowners. The most successful at this, in Woodbridge, were George and William Trott of Castle Street. Several vessels were registered as being under the ownership of Trott & Co, but, in fact, they only owned a percentage of the shares and acted as managers. These two master mariners held over half shares in the *Mary & Betsy*, built at Woodbridge in 1827 and finally wrecked off Holyhead in 1865. They managed the *Alexander* too, until she sank while on passage from

Middlesbrough to Ipswich, taking her crew down with her. Since the banker of the same name also had shares in her, presumably she had been named after him. Then there was *Perseverance*, formerly the *Ellen Catharionon*, which was sold to Grimsby in 1852, but had originally been a war prize. The other schooners registered to Trott & Co. were *Harriet*, *Flora*, *Laura* and *Richard & Sarah*, all built in the town and often trading to Liverpool. Also, someone in Woodbridge had owned the sloop *Liverpool*, but she was lost in a gale during 1840.

Woodbridge could, then, have been called a sailing ship town. Although being several miles from the sea, maritime activities touched almost everyone. The way in which capital was raised to build the schooners meant that most tradespeople were involved. Shares changed hands quite frequently. A schooner probably traded to and from the town for about forty years, during which time she fell under frequent changes of ownership. The master mariners held a highly esteemed position in local society, for it was on their ability that the town prospered. Also, there were mates, seamen and boys who manned the schooners. The town's shipwrights, if not building, were always patching the vessels up. There were two sailmakers at the Common Quay and also rope- and twine-makers, and there was a Swedish vice-consul and a Norwegian shipping agent to deal with the handling of cargoes.

Woodbridge was the port of registration for all vessels owned on the rivers Deben and Ore-Alde. At one time there were seventy vessels, totalling 5,000 tons, registered here. However, customs duty declined as the century grew older. In 1834 £2,263 was collected for the year; in 1844 it had gone up to £4,315, then nine years later it had gone down to £1,565. There were still over 20,000 tons a year 'going over the quays' at Woodbridge, but all was not well in this small Suffolk port. Shipbuilding stopped when a new source of timber became available to the world from the Canadian Atlantic coast. In the 1850s, local businessmen began to make use of this opportunity by acquiring two brigs (the 246 ton *Archibald* and the 95 ton *Bredaldare*), and also two brigantines (the 123 ton *Wallace* and the 156 ton *Antelope*). All were products of shipyards in Nova Scotia and New Brunswick.

On the end of a former Ferry Quay warehouse someone painted the eighteenth century Woodbridge Mariner. Its origins are unknown.

Getting schooners and brigs up to Woodbridge was a difficult and laborious task, to say nothing of tackling the shifting shingle banks and dangerous sand bar at the Deben entrance. Loaded schooners required ten to eleven feet of water and there was often insufficient water for them to get alongside the quays. Handling the clumsy schooners in confined waters meant frequent delays.

Probably the schooners' greatest drawback was the need for them to carry ballast to sail safely without a cargo. This meant that after discharging coal, forty tons of ballast had to be purchased in order for the vessel to sail back north to fetch more freight. At Woodbridge, sand cost three shillings a tumbrel load (half a ton). The ship's masters then had to spend time offloading the sand to a purchaser at the destination port, which probably just covered handling charges, and the process ate into the vessel's earning time.

The schooners had an unfortunate habit that played on the town's conscience – they would often sail off into the cold, grey North Sea and fail to make it back home.

In 1820, the sloop *Sarah & Caroline* ran up on the Newcome sand during a gale. The hulk sank and the crew of five took to the rigging. Luckily, the Lowestoft lifeboat reached them before they collapsed from exhaustion. The nine men on the schooner *Constant Trader* were not as fortunate when they ran onto the Cork Sand the following month. Again, the crew went up the rigging but conditions were so bad that no vessel could get near to take them off. Eventually, the power of the waves and flying spray tore them off, and one by one they fell into the sea.

The Woodbridge trading brigs and schooners certainly got around northern Europe. In 1854 the *Antelope*, owned by the Pretymans of Ramsholt Lodge, was lost trying to enter Hartlepool to shelter from a south-east gale. Unfortunately, a sunken vessel had blocked the harbour and the *Antelope* had been forced to go up on to the beach.

Over the years, the ships of Woodbridge met their end as they went about their normal occupation. In December 1884, the *Clementina* went ashore on the Goodwin Sands during a gale. Everyone on board, including the owner, was drowned. *Dorothea* met a similar fate on the Haisbro sand. The *Maria* foundered off Cromer whilst others, like *Archibald* and the Norwegian-built schooner *Ariel* (both from a number of schooners and cutters owned by Whyard of Orford) were lost at sea. They simply failed to arrive at their destinations. Generally, they didn't end up as hulks rotting in creeks; some were broken up for firewood and most fell foul of wind and sea and were lost off the coast.

Family hardship caused by the loss of men at sea did not pass unnoticed in a small community like Woodbridge. In 1840, a group of local maritime worthies met at the Anchor Inn and formed a society to give financial aid to the relatives of drowned seamen, and compensate for any gear they lost. Known as the Woodbridge Shipwreck Society, it lasted for nearly seventy years and in 1870 it had a reserve of £1,600. Most of the money was collected through donations from wealthy residents. The society had 163 members, and a voluntary committee carried out the business. George Trott was one of the founders, as was J. Dowsing, master of the *Dispatch*, and Mr Loft the boatbuilder.

Claims to the society varied. Aid was given to relatives of Will Marsh, who drowned after falling over the stern of the *Bernard Barton*, and Charles Bridge's family received recompense after he fell from the tops'l yard of the *Harriet* while the schooner was off Southwold. These men's relatives received pensions, but when George Pannifer was drowned while bathing off the coast off Portugal, in 1886, the committee did not think this was strictly within the ship's duty and his father only received half the normal compensation.

Quite a number of men came to grief in the shelter of the Deben estuary. Thomas Jackson was drowned off Kingston Quay when his punt upset as he was going off to the barge *Phoenia*. A seaman from *Flora* was drowned at Waldringfield. He had put the master ashore and was going back in the boat alone. Most schooners carried five hands and the committee expressed their strong opinion of the dangerous practice of permitting only one hand to accompany their master ashore, 'unless they be furnished with two small oars'. Presumably, the drowned seaman had been sculling the boat which, in spite of the strong opinion of the Shipwreck Society Committee, still remained the normal practice on barges and small coasters.

All too often, the committee had the duty of paying compensation after shipwrecks. The *Thetis*, under Captain John Bull, was wrecked in the Humber. Captain William Woodruffe survived after striking Sunderland's North Pier in the *Bee*, but was wrecked at Tees soon after, in the *Mary Ann*. The *Charlotte* was lost in the great gale of 1860, while the *James* sank at Harwich when on passage from Grimsby to Woodbridge carrying salt, and the *Harriet* founded on Dyck Bank off Dunkirk.

John How, master of the *Garland*, was paid four pounds for the loss of his charts, which had been 'destroyed in the dreadful gale at the time they were cutting away her masts in Drumore Bay.' It was a hard life combatting the sea in small, wooden sailing vessels and the Woodbridge schooners certainly made long voyages.

# SEVEN

# Sail to the End

In Tudor and Elizabethan times Woodbridge mushroomed up around the market and port. In the early stagecoach days, the London to Yarmouth highway came down Drybridge Hill and into Market Hill, but by the eighteen century the Thoroughfare had become the accepted main road.

The population of Woodbridge in 1801 was just over 3,000. The town prospered and by 1851 the count had risen to over 5,000. Then suddenly numbers began to drop as people moved away. However, the coming of the railways stabilised the situation until the 1930s. As various light industries grew up in Woodbridge, the figures began to increase again. Thus in 1959, when the *Woodbridge Reporter* celebrated its centenary, the town's population was almost the same as when the newspaper had been established. By 2016, numbers had risen to about 11,000 residents.

There had been a newspaper before the *Reporter*, but the *Woodbridge Advertiser*, started in 1843, had only appeared once a month whereas the Reporter was very much more up to date as it was a weekly. It must have been borne on a wave of optimism because it began in the same year as the railway line reached Woodbridge.

The history of the railway is really part of the national development and it ended the town's importance as a self-contained unit.

In 1794, one coach per day and a weekly wagon passed through the town on the way to London. The coach took thirteen hours to reach its destination. By 1844, twelve coaches, omnibuses, carrier's wagons and carts passed through the town each day with the journey to London taking five hours at a cost of ten shillings.

The railway did not meet with everyone's approval; many towns-people including the shipowner Cobbold and the landowner Col. Tomlin fought against it. Tomlin bought land and fenced it off to prevent development of the line, but later had a change of heart and helped the railway. A shed was erected where the line was going to be laid, but the railway company simple cut off one corner. There was anger when the East Suffolk Railway purchased the Waterside and Lime Kiln areas in 1856. A man named Smith was running a boatyard where the cinema now stands. This was all removed, as were the ancient saltpans where salt had been extracted by evapo-ration. Possibly the reason for situating the station so near the quays was because it was easier to get the track level on the flat ground alongside the Deben.

When the railway started, in 1859, many people believed this was the end of the town's usefulness as a port. In fact, commercial shipping continued for another seventy years and it was road transport that dealt the final knockout blow.

The shipowners and master mariners of Woodbridge must have watched with guarded enthusiasm as early locomotives hauled lines of loaded trucks into the station. As they walked home from chapel on Sundays, they must have discussed the situation in low tones about whether they could compete with those horrible, hissing engines that dragged goods into the town.

By this time a new kind of craft, spritsail barges, developed in the late eighteenth century, were being used in the Thames estuary. The first flat-bottomed barge owned on the Deben was the 50ft *Maria*, bought by Richard Osborne in 1844, probably to load coprolite. The Woodbridge mariners were totally unimpressed by barges and called them 'ditch crawlers.' They felt it was better to stick with the old tubby schooners than go to sea in sailing lighters. However, the barges saved money because they didn't have to take on ballast from the pit at Kyson Point every time they went to sea without a cargo.

In 1936 Dr Groom of Church Street started writing notebooks from the memories of old Woodbridge bargemen. Surprisingly, several of them referred to *Maria* of 1844 as being the first Woodbridge barge, although they must have been passing on their grandfather's memories of the river.

Not long after the *Maria* arrived, Jeremiah Read of Crown Place bought the barge *Eltham*. Read soon saw the advantages of barges and he moved on with the *Lady of the Wave*, one of the few barges on the Woodbridge register. In 1874 Read and the merchant G Ling had the round-sterned *Deben* built at Ipswich and she served Woodbridge for many years as a 'hoy', a packet running a regular service to London. Later, Read's sons skippered his barges – Arthur had the *Lady Ellen*, named after a daughter, and Fred had the *Deben*.

Another hoy running between the Thames and Woodbridge was the yawl *Hope*, owned by the grocers in the Thoroughfare and fitted with a tank to load household paraffin. She picked up food in London then loaded paraffin in Tilbury. She berthed at the Woodbridge Jetty, near the granary on stilts, and the boy had to pump the paraffin out of the tank by hand, then transfer it to another tank the other side of the river wall. Old Woodbridge men used to tell me that the *Hope* was abandoned just around the bend upriver of Sun Wharf and is still under the mud.

In 1883, 346 sailing ships and three steamers brought 22,968 tons to Woodbridge, which did not indicate a decline of its importance. Two years later there were 219 vessels registered here, but many of these were Aldeburgh and Orford craft, engaged in fishing. Woodbridge-registered craft gave employment to 350 men and boys. But by the mid-Victorian era, Woodbridge was struggling. The people of Woodbridge began to lose interest in the port, which was, after all, only a few tarred and weather-boarded warehouses standing on simply constructed quays, overlooking a little muddy estuary. Half the time it was just a wide expanse of mud with a few swans paddling around.

To get barges up to Woodbridge and Melton the first pilot had to guide them over the Deben bar and then another pilot boarded at Waldringfield. To get above Troublesome Reach three 'tidesmen' were hired to stand on the bow and pole the barges off the mud. To reach Melton Maltings and Wilford Bridge, a series of posts were

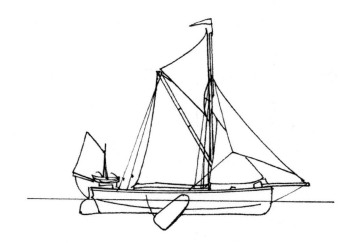

# SPRITSAIL BARGE ('SPRITTIE')
## 1835 – 1932

# KETCH BARGE ('BOOMIE')
## 1880 – 1923

FELIXSTOWE PILOT BOAT

TOPS'L SCHOONER
1830 - 1880

placed in the river above the Tide Mill to make it easier to swing the barges round the bends. All this added cost and delay to the cargoes.

The pilots had fast rowing boats, with a small sail, to operate in shallow waters. Pilot Sam Marsh had a new 12ft pilot boat built in a shed at the bottom of Brook Street in 1870, the same year that his son Ted was born. Ted became the last pilot and used the boat *Teddy* until she was put in a coal cellar under a Ferry Quay warehouse. After World War II, Frank Knights used the *Teddy* and then she went back in the cellar for well over 60 years. In 2007 I had the *Teddy* restored and she is now the oldest Woodbridge boat still afloat, and has taken part in rowing races at Maritime Woodbridge. Other Woodbridge boats were sold to Thorpeness Mere when it opened.

In 1879 a local printer called Loder was requested to pay a fine for libel, but the townspeople thought there had been a miscarriage of justice and organise a collection to settle the costs. Loder refused to take the money and said it should be used to dig Loder's Cut, a shortcut through a bend in the river which reduces the time it takes to get from Troublesome Reach to Kyson. The Cut is still in use by pleasure craft today.

Sailing barges, both spritsail and ketch-rigged 'boomies', quickly came to dominate the East Coast ports. Over the years they brought and took away thousands of tons of cargo from Woodbridge, yet very few were owned here or had local men as their skippers. 'Old' George Collins, of Ramsholt, told me that his father and uncles, like many men from coastal villages, had gone off into deep-sea square-riggers in the 1880s and 90s.

The seafaring Collins men liked to get about. One joined a clipper on the Australian run, while his father spent time in the South Pacific Isles on a trading schooner. After each voyage, they went back to their families in Suffolk. As I write, there are two ship models he gave me hanging on our wall. They had been waiting in his shed to be turned into firewood. Presumably, these were made to while away the off-watch time as the clippers ran back from Australia.

One of his uncles, also a George Collins, went 'a-bargin', and became mate on a boomie, trading more or less regularly to German ports. He brought a wife back on one trip and set up home near Sun Wharf. It cannot have been a soft job taking a flat-bottomed barge across the temperamental North Sea. The owners split the freight money with the crews, yet boomie mate Collins only averaged fifteen shillings a week and had to get parish relief to provide for his family.

In search of more space, the port of Woodbridge was extended upriver. Melton Dock was built in about 1794 for schooners working to the lime kiln there. Later a malt house and then maltings were built here. They needed cheap water transport, but there was also a railway track down to Melton Dock. There was a wooden granary on stilts beside the Dock, now under Simon Skeet's workshop. As the maltings does not seem to have been a success, it was converted into a 1,000 ton granary.

The New Quay was opened in 1846 just outside the Woodbridge boundary as an outlet for the brickfields and when these closed, the huge Melton Hill Maltings made use of the New Quay for cheap water transport. Wilford Bridge Wharf was built for the Suffolk County Council to bring in road-making material and, to make it quicker to get barges upriver a system of posts from the Tide Mill to Wilford Bridge allowed barges to be hauled round the bends in the upper reaches.

In two of Dr Groom's interviews there are accounts of a sad story of loss for Fred Finney from the 86ft boomie *Eastern Belle*, and I had heard the same story told by the blacksmith 'Chubby' Goldsmith. This sad event was probably a case of the flat-bottomed barge being pushed to the limit of her capability for economic reasons.

The *Eastern Belle* regularly brought coal from Scotland to the New Quay. It was looked on as an average voyage but must have been quite a demanding passage. Captain Finney had retired and handed over command of the *Eastern Belle* to his son Fred, but stayed on as mate. On the way back from Scotland they were 'below the Blyth' when, in

**The topsides being tarred on a Woodbridge trading ketch over on the Sutton Ferry Cliff beach.**

a fresh breeze, they had to gybe the barge. Old Captain Finney was on the wheel and young Captain Fred and a foreign seaman hauled in the mainsail. When the mainsail went over at speed, the seaman forgot to make the end of sheet fast and young Fred Finney was jerked off the deck and flung over the boom into the sea. His father at the wheel never saw his son come up but when the block was pulled in his severed fingers were still jammed in it. Captain Finney took the *Eastern Belle* into the Blyth and when Woodbridge heard about the tragedy the river community was deeply shocked.

Old mariners were justified in calling early barges 'ditch crawlers' and in mistrusting their ability to make sea passages. One of these local barges was the *Bengal* of Woodbridge. The dry facts that have survived about this vessel are that she had a topping up bowsprit and had been built at Ipswich in 1857.

The boomie (ketch) barge *Sussex Belle* at Tide Mill Quay in about 1910. She regularly traded to Woodbridge and Orford with coal from Keadby.

In the autumn of 1967, I took the ocean racer *Giselle of Iken* away from Snape quay. The Alde pilot, 'Jumbo' Ward had just brought up the coaster *Gillation* with a cargo of 250 tons, the first imported freight from Europe during George Gooderham's ownership of Snape Maltings. Jumbo then piloted us downriver and the conversation turned to barges owned by Newson Garrett. Jumbo talked about events of a hundred years before, that he had heard from his grandfather, as if they had taken place just a few months earlier.

Jumbo Ward's grandfather, 'Ducker' Ward, went to sea on the Margaret in 1859 at the age of nine, but he was not allowed to lift a hot kettle off the stove. This 35-ton cutter was engaged in carrying ammunition from Hamburg to British ports. Once, while on passage from London to Snape, young Ducker Ward shouted to the skipper that there was a whale on the Buxey sand. The skipper shook his head. 'No boy, that's no whale, that's a barge's chine.' Sure enough, it was in fact, the *Bengal*, floating bottom upwards while all her crew had been drowned. Apparently, when she'd been built money had been tight and the yard owner had laid off his workers but, as he was bound to pay his apprentices, they had constructed the *Bengal* 'on spec'. Unfortunately, the boys turned out a barge that was wider across the bottom than at deck level. The *Bengal*'s career had been comparatively short and her stability had always been doubtful.

In about 1923 the boomie barge *Sussex Belle* brought coal from Allerton Main colliery to Sun Wharf and this was probably her last cargo into the Deben. The 86ft boomie *Empress of India*, under Captain Douse, ran for many years as a collier, carrying coal from Seaham to the Tide Mill Quay. For a return freight some barges loaded a mixture called 'mill wash', that was used for road-making. The other return freights followed the old schooner practice of loading shingle from the Deben Bar, which was sold in the North of England for the construction of new docks. The barges ran alongside the shingle knolls or on the Bawdsey beach just below the Quay, or on the Felix-stowe Ferry side, and the fishermen loaded them. Many thousands of tons of shingle were removed from the Deben and Shingle Street river entrances until just after World War II. Shingle was also taken from Landguard Point up to Ipswich until about 1970 in the barge *Melissa*.

Surprisingly, one tops'l schooner, the *English Rose*, still made a frequent appearance in the small ports of Suffolk. Once, many years ago, the *English Rose* was wind-bound (wind in the wrong direction to leave port) in Yarmouth Roads and her skipper 'wired' for his girlfriend to come up from Dover. While the lady was travelling, a fair wind sprang up, but the schooner stayed at anchor and the rest of the southbound fleet sailed on. At last, the girlfriend arrived and the *English Rose* continued her leisurely way to Dover. Here, the girlfriend's sister came aboard and the skipper invited her to share the aft cabin as he took a fancy to her. The result was an almighty row between the sisters and, in a great frenzy, the original girlfriend threw herself overboard. Her sister followed her closely. Neither of them could swim. The skipper jumped into the schooner's boat and managed to save his favourite sister. After the inquest, the skipper

The Ferry Dock, Woodbridge in about 1912
with nine barges.

and sister were married on the same day and they sailed off on the evening tide towards the north, for another load of coal.

As she drew 11ft (3.6m) of water the *English Rose* sometimes had to wait two weeks before trying to get up to Ferry Quay in Woodbridge. Then they had sixteen men on her windlass and literally dragged her through the mud so that she was a foot above her marks. To reach

Lime Kiln Quay she had to have thirty tons taken out of her into a lighter at Sutton Ferry.

Jim Lewis was skipper of the boomie *Laura*. Once, when anchored at Ramsholt, he walked to his home at Boyton, leaving two Shottisham boys on the barge. That night, the boys stoked up the foc'sle fire and turned in for a good night's sleep. Both being sound sleepers, they did not hear a westerly gale spring up. With that, a spring tide, and the fact there was not enough chain out, they woke to find the barge high and dry up against the saltings. When skipper Lewis returned, he had some very hard words of practical advice to give his crew. Not that it made any difference, for the barge had to stay there for a fortnight, until the next spring tide, when she floated and continued on up to Woodbridge.

In the days when every tide carried a barge up to Woodbridge, a man who 'ran away to sea' was Arthur Hunt. He was the son of Sir Cuthbert Quilter's head gamekeeper and, unbeknown to his parents, he signed up to work on a boomie that happened to be discharging coal at Ramsholt Dock. After this, he went on up to Woodbridge in the barge to help them finish unloading. Arthur's parents walked six miles to plead with him to come home. In the end, after failing to persuade their son with all the arguments over the follies of a sailor's life, they provided him with sufficient clothing to help him on his way. Later, he joined Parker's barges, first as a mate, then as skipper of the *Dover Castle*. He also joined the racing crew of the *Violet Sybil*. Following a disagreement with Clem Parker, he left and joined the Fowey schooner *Alert*, at Ipswich. During the First World War he went into steam ships, but after a lung injury he returned to his home estuary, the Deben.

Arthur acquired the philosophical outlook of a man trained in sailing ships, and thus developed a considerable talent for telling a yarn. Arthur was the last professional yacht skipper on the Deben. In the winter, the yacht *Genesta* was laid up against the broken-down barge quay. In her cabin, Arthur made nets for Aldeburgh fishermen and weekend trawler men. I spent many hours, during my school holidays, sitting in the cabin listening to yarns about the 'old days'.

He was glad of someone to talk to, as he worked away at his trawls in the snug little cabin. His face was weather-beaten to a walnut colour but the top of his forehead, where his cap went, was always white.

One thing Arthur gave me was his father's recipe for poisoning rats. I was solemnly presented with a very faded piece of paper on which, dating back to the 1880s, a Norwich chemist had written a reliable rat-killing bait. It had been treasured by the Hunt family until there were no longer any gamekeepers and it was passed on to me. I was very flattered but never dared put Hunt's poison into action. It started off harmlessly with, 'one peck of fine barley meal, sifted', but the real knockout ingredient, arsenic, is capable of killing every living creature for miles around.

How I wish I had written down some of the stories that Arthur Hunt told me. Perhaps the best tale concerned the fate of one of Mr Bloss's bullocks. In about 1912 the *Pacific*, one of Goldsmith's of Grays steel barges, was tied up at Melton Dock when its skipper and mate discovered that they had developed that recurring human phenomenon – they had spent all their money. Perhaps this was a common occurrence for this pair. Perhaps they could not get a 'sub' from the owners. In this unhappy state, they sat on the barge's fore hatch with nothing else to look at but a bunch of Mr Bloss's fat cattle grazing on one of his Melton marshes beyond.

Now, the mate of this barge had, at one time, been a butcher's assistant and he must have been the prime mover of that night's dishonest work. They drove a bullock up onto the dock, roped it up and killed it, in the old poleaxe manner. In the darkness, they bled the animal into the ebb tide, and then, by lamplight, they cut the carcass up in the hold. Next, they went up to Wilford Bridge where three of Parker's barges were discharging stone. After waking up the crews, the entrepreneurs sold some of their ill-acquired meat. They did the same at the Ferry Dock and, by dawn, every barge in the upper reaches of the Deben had parts of the missing animal hidden aloft, in their tops'ls.

Strange to say, this crime was never detected, although the police must have had a shrewd idea of what became of the bullock. The following midday, a policeman went into the Boat Inn and began questioning all the bargemen and riverside workers who were in there playing quoits. Reputedly, one constable even remarked that he could smell an extremely good joint in the oven. Never has such an obvious clue been so casually overlooked.

In the last days of Woodbridge as a port, Horlock's steel barge *Repertor* was almost sunk at the Tide Mill Quay. Flat-bottomed barges were rather prone to creating suction in the mud, and when this occurred, they weren't able to float with the tide. It didn't happen often, although Hythe Quay at Colchester was noted for it. In the case of *Repertor*, her skipper was just turning in for the night when he noticed his barge was not rising with the tide. As quickly as possible, they put the hatches on and caulked up all the deck openings. Usual methods of breaking the suction were tried, but it was not until the deck was under water, up to the bottom of the wheel, that *Repertor* suddenly lurched up and shook herself free of the mud.

There was a countdown to the extinction of trading on the river. No longer did barges bring malting barley up to Ferry Dock to be taken by horse and cart to Brook's Crown Maltings. Thomas Damant, manager of Ipswich Malting Co.'s Melton Hill Malting, had bought the *Lady Ellen*, but the last cargoes that came to the New Dock were probably in the early 1920s. The *Edith May* brought wheat to the Tide Mill in about 1926. Frank Knights, then a young boy living in Melton, thought that Horlock's *Reminder* had been the last barge to Melton Dock in about 1931.

Some time early in the last century, Captain Robert Skinner had begun to play a part in the maritime affairs of Woodbridge. He had been master of the large schooner barges *Zebrina* and *Belmont* that were owned by the Whitstable Shipping Co. Then Skinner started on his own, as part-owner of the boomie *Lord Alcester* in which the coal merchant Cox also had a share. The Deben seemed a good place, then, to establish a barge-owning enterprise. After all, there was no one else attempting it. Skinner's method of retailing coal was to sell it

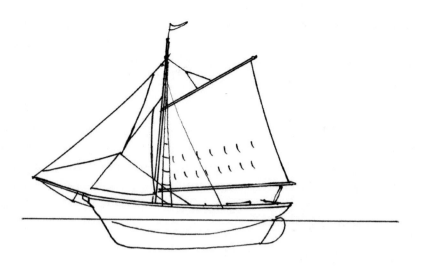

# TRADING SLOOP  1770-1830

# WOODBRIDGE PILOT BOAT

straight out of the barge, in small amounts. It was easier for the village people to buy it at riverside quays than to collect it from Woodbridge or Melton stations. Word went round when Skinner was in the river, and anyone wanting coal took a horse and tumbrel, or even just a wheelbarrow, down to the waterside to buy some.

In 1968, Skinner's son George told me that he had come right up to the jetty on his father's barge *Lord Alcester* with 290 tons of coal. Here Skinner and Cox had a small shop retailing coal straight to the public.

The time it took barges to get up the Deben had not mattered in the Edwardian period, but commerce began to move faster in the 1920s. The *Lord Alcester* was sold and Skinner bought the boomie *Lord Hartington*, but a German cargo liner ran her down in the West Schelde River in 1928. Skinner then bought small spritty *Dover Castle* and picked up a modest living running shingle from the Deben entrance up to Wilford Bridge.

Captain Skinner's three sons joined his barge enterprise. John skippered the *Lord Hartington* until he took a job in North Woolwich, Wesley was mate with his father in the *Lord Alcester* and later owned the *Martin Luther* and the *Nautilus*. George, the youngest son of this sea-going family, first 'went away' in the barge *Zebrina* when she was rigged as a barquentine. Later, he came to Woodbridge to help with the family coal business, but he could not settle and went off again aboard steamers. He became a quartermaster with P&O and then changed to the continental ferry service from Harwich, before he eventually came back to barges. He took the *Dover Castle*, which was not a coasting barge, up to the Humber, after coal, but preferred taking the *Lord Alcester* to the Tyne, loading her with coal and heading to the Biscay ports. This barge carried five hands and an average passage lasted nine or ten days. After this, he joined Cranfield's Ipswich grain barges as skipper of the Venture for quite a while. But he did not like spritty barges; they were never out of sight of land for long enough. He told me all this while waiting to row people across on the Woodbridge Ferry to Sutton.

Captain Robert Skinner dumped the *Dover Castle* on the mud under Sutton Ferry Cliff and carried on transporting shingle in his

*Tuesday*. It was said that Skinner was never paid for the shingle he brought up for the new bypass. The *Tuesday* was in a poor state and she drifted up and down on the tide with her sails in pieces. It must have been a sad blow for the old captain.

At eighty-two, Skinner was sailing down to Felixstowe Ferry by himself and going alongside the beach. Then, in one tide, local men from the Ferry used to barrow 90 tons of shingle into the barge. In 1935 the Ferry men noticed the *Tuesday* had been at anchor for several days with no sign of life. Pilot Billy Newson and Charlie Brinkley rowed out to the barge and found Skinner dead in his bunk.

About this time, Harold Smy was on his father's barge *Cryalls*, taking shingle to the Suffolk County Council's Wilford Wharf. Harold recalled the Deben was an 'easy river' because the pilots, Ted Marsh and Nelson Oxborrow, were so good. The Woodbridge pilots rowed downriver to Waldringfield and watched for a barge's tops'l as they came upriver. To get to Woodbridge with a head wind, 'tides men' used to stand on the barge's bows with long poles and push them off the mud.

Adeline Thomson's father had the Railway Tavern, now the Wilford Bridge pub, and she used to look out of her window and watch the sails of the barges coming closer to Wilford Wharf with sand and stone. She also knew the bargemen and told me about her memories of them – one was called Jim had a dog, and another skipper accidentally shot his eye out with his poaching shotgun. In 1938 Basil Brown and his fellow Sutton Hoo diggers used to come in to the pub for a 'pot of beer,' but barges had stopped coming by then.

Small steamers had traded into the river, and it was easier for them to keep in the channel. The steamer *River Witham* came to Woodbridge regularly in the early 1930s and there was an attempt to start a fleet of motor coasters based at Sun Wharf. The dredger *Justice* also operated from here. This wharf was bought by the Woodbridge Canning Co., who had coal brought in by steamers and dried peas (for canning) by Dutch coasters.

The last commercial cargo to Woodbridge was coal for Sun Wharf in the steamer *Maloo* in the hard winter of 1940. She had to wait at Waldringfield for ice to clear in the river before pilot Ted Marsh

The Thames Sailing Barge *Centaur* approaching Tide Mill Quay in 2012.

124

could bring her up. The endless delays made sea cargoes too expensive at Woodbridge.

However, the pilots at Felixstowe Ferry were the ones who really ended the port. They had been happy to bring barges drawing 6ft (2m) in, but the coasters were drawing 12ft (4m) in a channel that was only just 4m deep. The pilots used to hear them scraping the bottom when coming over the Bar at the entrance and refused to bring in any more in as they knew that one day a ship would get into difficulties there. Frank Knights recalled that until the early 1930s, barge trade was going on normally and it took a long time for people to realise that no more barges were coming. Just after World War II the river was more or less deserted. There were very few people about. Hervey Benham, writing in his barge book 'Down Tops'l' in 1951 referred to the Deben as being a 'yachtsman's paradise'. He hit the nail on the head.

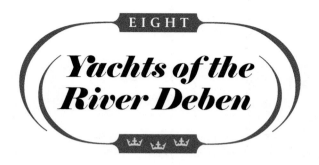

# EIGHT

# Yachts of the River Deben

Leisure boating has been long established on Suffolk's rivers. In 1758 a 21ft pleasure-sailing boat was auctioned at 'Orford Key.' In June of 1784, the *Temple* and the *Flora* raced from the Common Quay, Woodbridge, to Bawdsey Ferry and back for a 'valuable' silver cup. After this, there was a lunch at the Queen's Head. This event had captured the attention of the newspaper reporter because some unsporting character had stolen one of the contesting craft. There was quite a fuss, but it looks as though the stolen boat was eventually returned. However, it appears that this was the first recorded mention of racing on the river at Woodbridge. Racing of one sort or another has been going on, more or less continuously, ever since.

The Deben Yacht Club has its origins in the Woodbridge Regatta, held in 1838 to mark Queen Victoria's Coronation. Seven yachts took part in a sailing race, while gigs came from other Suffolk rivers to take part in the rowing races. A small nucleus of yachts were kept on moorings downriver of the Ferry Dock. Among these were the *Rival*, the *Syren* and the *Pearl*. In about 1830 the *Helen* made a pleasure cruise to Holland from Woodbridge. The shipbuilders must have been responsible for many of the local yachts. William Taylor built the *Osprey* and others, no doubt. Garrard built a six-oared galley 'for gentlemen to row'. In 1854, there was a purse of three pounds for the winner of the eighteen-foot-skiff rowing event. Four-oared boats shared a purse of ten sovereigns, seven for first place and three for second.

Rowing was a popular pastime at Woodbridge and Ipswich until after World War I and several shopkeepers in the town had open rowing boats. On Sunday, families used to row on the river, always

**Waldringfield Regatta in 1924 with barge *Dover Castle* as the committee boat.**

working it so that they went with the tide. The rapid increase in the introduction of motorboats in the 1920s made rowing old-fashioned and people lost interest. The old Woodbridge Rowing Club appears to have kept its boats at Robertsons yard where the boats lay abandoned until about 1954 when Bert Robertson decided to clear the old boats out of his shed and burn them. In 1992, Terry Davey started to organise rowing events based at Felixstowe Ferry Sailing Club. This grew into the Deben Rowing Club, which moved upriver to Woodbridge and, in 2010, the new clubhouse and boat store were built on the River Wall. By 2017, this club had about 130 members who mainly used the Deben for recreation and training and travelled to other clubs to take part in racing events.

The 19th century method of handicapping yachts in the regatta was to allow half a minute for every ton above twelve tons. In the small class, the same system applied for every ton above six. The yachts competed for a purse of ten sovereigns, plus five shillings. It was all very simple, but no doubt there were arguments! In the evening there

The Deben Rowing Club's Daughters of the Deben rowed up the river and back before taking the boat up to Sutton Hoo led by Josh Sayle, Mayor of Woodbridge, 2015.

was a dinner at the Crown, followed by a fete and a fireworks display on the bowling green. In 1872 the annual river event was enlarged and called the Grand Woodbridge Regatta, with the usual festivities in the town afterwards. In 1886 a meeting was held at the Crown and it was agreed to turn the Regatta committee into the Deben Sailing Club. This group appears to have administered the Regatta and also held frequent sailing and rowing matches. In the 1930s it also organised swimming races in Robertsons tidal swimming pool at the Lime Kiln yard.

Swimming had become popular at Woodbridge in the final years of Queen Victoria's reign, but of course as men swam naked, proprieties had to be observed so men swam in one part of the river and women swam separately, out of sight of male eyes. How quickly attitudes changed! In the 1930s, diving exhibitions by both men and women were being given to the paying public at Robertson's pool.

Woodbridge Swimming Gala in 1934 at Robertsons. In about 1912 Robertsons dug a swimming pool with a mud bottom and used tidal water. In 1940 the pool was closed because some soldiers became ill after using it.

Edward FitzGerald is the nineteenth century yachtsman we know most about. He was a yachtsman in the Victorian sense, which meant that he didn't actually take part in the sailing of the boat. Paid hands did this, with a professional skipper at the wheel who made the decisions. FitzGerald was, to all intents and purposes, a passenger. He owned nine different craft at various times, the best known being the 14 ton schooner *Scandal*, which was built at Wivenhoe in 1863. FitzGerald claimed she was named after the main product of Woodbridge. He sold the schooner to Sir Cuthbert Quilter, who had little time for humour and renamed her *Sapphire*.

Quilter's steam yacht *Peridot* anchored in Cross Reach. The *Peridot* had a deep draft and was anchored because she couldn't get further up the river. The crew had to row ashore and walk up to Woodbridge Station, then carry the luggage for the guests for Bawdsey Manor.

It may seem odd that two men with such widely different personalities led yachting in the Deben. FitzGerald was a brilliant, if slightly eccentric, literary gentleman; while Quilter was a pillar of the local establishment, a much respected and very capable man. He also took on *Scandal*'s master, Captain Ablett Passiful. This yachtmaster went on to command a long line of craft for Quilter. The largest yachts were the 110 ton *Foam* and the 171 ton Zoe. In the seasons of 1874–75, Passiful took the yawl *Hirondelle* round the coast, racing in all the large regattas. Later, he commanded the steam yachts *Firefly* and *Peridot*. The home port registered for these yachts was Cowes (which was the correct place for a gentleman to keep his yacht), but they spent quite a lot of time laying in the Deben off Bawdsey Manor. When Quilter represented South Suffolk in the House of Commons, the 43 TM-ton (Thames Measurement, one of the many standards by which to measure a ship) *Peridot* often lay in the Thames, and many prominent statesmen joined him on his steam yacht for a voyage to Bawdsey. No doubt Bawdsey Manor made a welcome sight from the elegant *Peridot* when she rounded Walton-on-the-Naze with smoke pouring out of her slender funnel. By then Quilter had given up his house in Portsmouth and the *Peridot* was based at Bawdsey, laid up in the winter in the entrance of Bawdsey Fleet.

When the weather was not suitable, or time was pressing, Quilter went upriver and caught the train at Woodbridge. The *Peridot* drew 6ft and was sometimes held up in the upper reaches, so that the term 'caught the train' was not quite correct. In fact, the stationmaster kept the train waiting until Quilter arrived. There was even a special gate made so that he could reach the platform easily.

The revival of wooden boatbuilding at Woodbridge began when Ebenezer Robertson took over the Lime Kiln Yard. Also known as 'Khartoum' Robertson, he was of Scots descent, wore the kilt and played the bagpipes when he felt so inclined. He already had St Peter's Shipyard at Ipswich, where he built the barquentine *Uncle Ned* in 1867, which was still afloat at Arklow in 1940.

The boomie barge *Nanita*, built by Robertson in 1880, nearly paid for herself in two years, but after this there was a drop in barge incomes and Ebenezer changed over to building yachts. Ebenezer had property in Southwold and had seen the empty Lime Kiln Yard from the train when he went through to collect his rents. He bought it in 1884 to develop yacht building, although barges were also repaired here. Ebenezer sold the old patent slip to a Rochester firm, and removed the grids where large vessels had previously come up to be scrubbed. Every Monday, he arrived by train from Ipswich to inspect the progress at Lime Kiln before continuing on to Southwold.

Ebenezer's son, A.V. Robertson, came over to Woodbridge to run the yard when he was eighteen, and was later responsible for that curious local phenomenon, the barge yacht. This was an attempt to translate the successes of the large, cargo-carrying spritties into cruising yachts. The driving force of this movement was the Burnham-on-Crouch yachtsman E.B. Tredwen who designed them. He saw, quite correctly, that deep-keeled yachts were quite useless for the East Coast and, instead, he pioneered the flat-bottomed, unballasted barge yacht. The idea caught on, and a number were built around the East Coast. Robertson made a speciality of them including the 25ft *Venus* that was sailed to the Baltic. In 1904, Robertson built the 29ft *Nan* that cruised to Berwick-on-Tweed, and the 35ft *Pearl*, launched, complete with a piano. Unfortunately, she was destroyed by fire whilst on the Clyde.

It was realised that the behaviour at sea of the small, boxy, gaff-rigged barge yachts left quite a lot to be desired, and that a greater part of the spritties' success had been due to their size. Barge yachts were then built larger and, in some cases, the same size as their trading counter-parts. Howard, the famous Maldon barge-builder, produced the 80ft *Thoma II* in 1909 and, two years later, the 40ft *Lady Frances* for his own use. Robertson's contribution was the lovely sprits'l rigged *Esnia*, which was slightly larger than *Lady Frances*. She was designed by GU Laws and built at the Lime Kiln Yard in 1909 on a piece of ground just round the corner from the dock. No owner kept *Esnia* for more than three years but despite being slow, some of the barge yachts like her lasted for three quarters of a century and without capsizing, as their critics always claimed they would.

The barge yachts were quite popular at Woodbridge because at low tide they would sit on the mud without falling over. A number were kept here, including the *Heron*. The last one built here was the 18 ton ketch, *Marietta*, built in 1916. I remember going on board her in the early 1950s, when she was laid up at Waldringfield. I was shown the novel 'heads' situated in the bottom drawer of a cupboard in the main saloon.

When a boy at the Woodbridge School, the Reverend William Groom used to go down and watch the progress as the hull of the Marietta was being built at Robertsons. In about 1954, he bought her and had a Bermudan mast installed. The Marietta caused something of a sensation in early 1967 when she sank at her mooring off Ramsholt Dock, on the same day that her owner passed away.

The Lime Kiln Yard was taken on by Bert Robertson, A.V. 'Robbie' Robertson's son and during the 1930s they were turning out a four-ton-class of yacht designed by Captain O.M. Watts. They cost £175 new, and £220 with a Stuart Turner engine fitted. This transom-sterned class was called the Ranzo. The counter-sterned version known as Mrs Ranzo was a little beamier. After Bert Robertson retired, the business was sold and regular wooden boatbuilding stopped at the Lime Kiln Yard. By the mid-1960s, A.V. Robertson Ltd was chiefly concerned with fitting the interiors into the fibreglass hulls of the 25ft Wing class yacht. When Mike Illingworth ran Robertsons Boatyard, they built several new boats, but having the all-important slipway for getting boats out of the water, their main concern was with repairs.

When Ebenezer reopened the Lime Kiln Yard, it was intended that his son-in-law, A.A. Everson, and his son A.V. Robertson would go into partnership, but this did not materialize. Instead, in 1886, Ebenezer started Everson off in a separate boatbuilding business situated at the Jetty, at the bottom of the Avenue where Ebenezer also ran a coal merchant's business.

In 1923 Everson built the *Dream*, an open sailing boat designed to be hauled up on Aldeburgh beach. She proved popular and later had a cabin fitted. A slightly larger 3 ton yacht called the *Cherub* was built on the same lines. This proved to be the beginning of the *Cherub* class of yachts, originally costing £125 and suitable for local estuary cruising.

The *Cherub*'s round bow design was also used on the gaff yacht *Clytie* that Everson built in 1922. Later, the original round bow was replaced by a 6ft extended bow, and her rig was altered from gaff to bermudian. Reg Browne kept *Clytie* at Everson's for decades. Every spring, the sight of the white-sailed yacht, traversing the empty grey waters of the Deben on her first weekend cruise, heralded the opening of the sailing season. In the autumn, when all the other yachts had been laid up, *Clytie* was still being sailed. When she stopped appearing, winter really had arrived.

In 1992, Paul and Jo Masters had the *Clytie*'s extended bow removed to return her to her original hull shape with a gaff cutter rig. Jo is the fifth member of her family to have owned *Clytie*, and this boat is the longest resident yacht on the Deben.

⚓

The internal combustion engine had the same revolutionary effect on vessels afloat as it did on road vehicles. The early marine engines

Paul and Jo Master's *Clytie* taking part in the Parade of Sail to mark 25 years of the River Deben Association, 2015. The *Clytie* was built by Eversons in 1922 and is the longest resident yacht on the Deben, owned mostly by one family.

were monsters, of uncertain temper. Quite a number of yachtsmen would have nothing to do with them. Probably the first full-powered craft on the Deben was the decked-in launch *Monare*, built in 1902. In roughly the same period, 'Robbie' Robertson had a similar craft called the Daimler, named after her inboard Daimler engine. She was used for passenger-carrying trips. The barge yacht *Esnia* had been fitted with a paraffin Gardner when she was launched in 1909. By the 1920s, an 'iron tops'l' was a normal fitting. Many people who messed about in boats in those far off days carried permanent scars as a memorial to the time when their primitive yacht engines had backfired or exploded in some unexpected manner while they tried to coax them into life.

For all their uncertainties, the combustion engine in small cars gave yachtsmen the opportunity to drive to places with anchorages further down the Deben. Here their yachts could lay afloat all the time, instead of spending half their lives perched on the Woodbridge mud. They discovered deserted waterside villages and a quiet, peaceful estuary. However it did not remain that way for long. Waldringfield was the first place to attract people, since it offered the best anchorage. Small rowing and dinghy sailing events were held at Waldringfield before the First World War, but the first proper regatta was held in 1920, and the following year Waldringfield Sailing Club was formed. There was no looking back after that. The sailing club at Felixstowe Ferry started the same way, with a small event every year in which local people and a few holidaymakers had sailing and rowing races in heavy, clinker dinghies. These events eventually blossomed into the original Felixstowe Yacht and Dinghy Club which became Felixstowe Ferry Sailing Club.

With the growth in yachting came more work for yacht builders. In the 1920s, Nunn Bros took over the quay at the old Waldringfield cement factory and began boatbuilding there. In the late sixties, the yard was still run by one of the founders, Ernie Nunn and they had a good name for Dragon-class building, supplying owners all over the country. The tradition of wooden boat construction spread to such an extent that, in the sixties, there were eight places on the Deben where it was possible to have a sizeable wooden boat built. As Waldringfield is an isolated village, Mike Nunn left the yard in 1961 and opened the Seamark Nunn chandlery at Trimley St Martin, which had the advantage of main road access. In 2013, Andrew Nunn received the Marine Retailer of the Year Award at the International Boat Show, London.

The best-known yard on the Deben was, unquestionably, Whisstocks Boatyard Ltd. Claude Whisstock went to sea in steamships just after the First World War. But during the Depression, as it was hard to get a berth on a ship, he did a spell at Robertsons with the objective of eventually becoming a ship's carpenter. From there, he went on to work for Brook Marine at Lowestoft. This job finished abruptly during the 1926 General Strike when Brooks had a 'lock out'. Claude Whisstock returned to Woodbridge and took on jobs repairing boats, but this activity went slowly, and his main source of income had been running motorboat trips at the weekends. He used to take day-trippers to Felixstowe Ferry and back, for 'eighteen pence a head'.

There was limited access to the waterside at Woodbridge and the only site Claude could find was a piece of marsh behind Ferry Dock Quay. His first workshop was built on stilts and the marsh was gradually filled in. However the ooze mud in front of the yard always made it a difficult place to launch a yacht into the river.

One of Claude's early jobs was to patch up the barge *Nautilus*. She was being poked up the river to Melton Dock when she got stuck on a post in Hackney Reach. As the tide went down, the post rose up through her bottom. Fortunately, as the barge's timbers were a bit 'ripe' they didn't crack and the post fitted tightly without letting a drop of water in. When Claude and 'Bow' Wilson went up to carry out repairs, they found that it was a piece of witch elm, in perfect condition. They sawed off the top, and then the bottom piece which was outside the barge, and told the skipper that it was best left there, as it was a far sounder piece of timber than any other in the barge.

The first sizeable craft to be built by Whisstocks was the 35ft motor cruiser *Bendor*, built in 1932. After this came the passenger carriers *Ocean Viking* and *Orwell Viking*. These were followed by a series of wooden Thames launches, lifeboat tenders and other small vessels. One of Claude's unusual jobs was to help fit out the fully rigged ship, *Joseph Conrad*, at Cliff Quay, Ipswich in 1934. The entire workforce from the yard went over and lived aboard this square-rigger and, later, Alan Villiers invited Claude Whisstock to go as a 'chippy' on the world cruise, but by then he had too many ties ashore.

In 1937, the first Deben four-tonner was launched, designed by William Maxwell Blake. He was a Woodbridge man who had been in charge of a naval dockyard in the Far East before retiring to Felix-

The barge *Deben* having a new tops'l
stretched while laying off the mud ooze
which became Whisstock's yard. Owned by
Read of Crown Place the *Deben* was built in
1875. This view was taken from Sutton Ferry
path. Sutton children still used to cross on
the ferry to go to the New Street School
after World War II.

stowe. Until then, Woodbridge had relied on London and Burnham-
on-Crouch naval architects and had been rather removed from the
initial creative force needed for yacht construction. Maxwell Blake
produced a number of designs during the thirties, notably *Mirelle*,
which was built by Whisstocks for Philip Allen. As buyers for the
Deben four-tonners were quickly found, Maxwell Blake designed a
Deben six-tonner. The last Maxwell Blake 'one off" yacht from the
yard was the *Florence Edith*. Claude Whisstock designed the 46ft
motor cruiser *Reda* which, apart from the smaller boats constructed
on the yard, was the only craft to have been designed by him.

By the time the World War II started, Whisstocks had become

the prime boatbuilding yard in Woodbridge. The war years saw over 200 small craft for various uses built here for the War Department, Admiralty and Ministry of Transport. After the war, everything was rationed and the yard had to concentrate on building fishing boats because wood permits were only available for commercial craft. However, in 1946 two Deben four-tonners left the yard, and the following year saw a gradual change back to yachts. In 1948, the Deben four-tonner *Wren* was built for Percy Woodcock and the *Carte Blanche* for Geoffrey Ingram-Smith. By then, this class was being sold to owners in the USA, Canada and Spain.

'Jack' Francis Jones of Waldringfield qualified as a naval architect in

1941, but spent the war years in naval coastal forces and was invalided out in 1945. Among his many designs was the 46ft, 26 ton gaff cutter *Corista*, built by Whisstocks for Philip Allen in 1952. She was an exceptionally handsome craft with a very bold sheer and was one of the finest of her type ever produced.

By 1954, the demand for Deben four-tonners had ceased. By then, 54 had been completed. Whisstocks did build one more, in 1960, for an American who had lost his original four-tonner in hurricane Carol. The replacement was built in teak and should, therefore, last indefinitely. In 1956 they built the 4.5 ton *Phialle*, which was the first yacht to be built to a design by Kim Holman and was for his own use. Five years later, the same designer produced a yard stock-boat, the 26ft Holman 26, which was followed, shortly afterwards, by the Holman 50.

It is very difficult to pick out a pattern but, to begin with, Whisstocks built any kind of craft that was ordered. After World War II they built small cruising yachts, then 'one off' upmarket yachts. They built the 'racing machine' *Breeze of Yorkshire*, intended for the One Ton Cup; the Maurice Griffith designed 17 ton ketch *Good Hope*, with balustrade round her high stern; and the J. Francis Jones designed, 9.5 ton diesel ketch *Gingerbread*. Practically the only bare hull brought to the yard for completion was that owned by the best-selling author Hammond Innes, the *Mary Deare*. She had been built of steel in Holland and brought to Woodbridge for fitting out. The gaff rig still appealed to some owners on the East Coast, and some of the last Whisstocks yachts were given that rig.

Woodbridge was a successful boatbuilding centre until the production of fibreglass suddenly saw the number of yachts rocket upwards. In about 1964, the first fibreglass yacht arrived at Ferry Quay. Claude Whisstock and Frank Knights waited until everyone had gone home and then climbed aboard to look at her. Frankly, they were both appalled and could not see how this type of yacht could last. They both decided to go on building wooden hulls.

Frank Knights (Shipwrights) tried to revive wooden boat building. In 1990 they built the 19ft Dunwich longshore fishing boat *Dodger*,

Claude Whisstock and Ted Marsh sailing *Cyrela* towards the yard in October 1939. Photograph courtesy of the Whisstock family and *A History of Whisstock's Boatyard* (2017).

then the open launch *Regardless* in 1992 followed by a similar open boat the following year. In 1994 they built my 18ft *Three Sisters*, based on the original 1888 Southwold longshore fishing boat hull. Knights made a final attempt to build wooden boats with the 14ft Kingfisher *Capercaillie* in about 1998, but the economics of wooden boatbuilding just no longer stacked up. The yard continued repairing boats and engines until Frank and his partner Keith Cutmore retired and the yard closed in 2002.

Whisstocks carried on building wooden hulls, but found it increasingly difficult to get orders as fibreglass became more accepted. Eventually there were not enough orders to maintain a staff and Whisstocks closed in 1984. The yard and yachts in it were seized but one of the boatowners bought the yard so that he didn't lose his new yacht. The yard reopened, run by Claude's son George and larger sheds were built. I remember walking past the morning it reopened and seeing George, sweeping the slipway down and whistling happily.

Fibreglass was still an unpopular word on the Woodbridge water-side and the yard switched over to building aluminium hulls. They launched *Rum 'n' Ginger* in 1990 and then *Windward Dream*. Sadly, this was not to last, and eventually the yard closed and 32 people lost their jobs.

Martin Wenyard then rented the yard. He reopened it and bought a powerful winch from Cromer lifeboat station to haul out large boats. An important order had been to upgrade the passenger-carrying motor ketch *Deben Glen* but sadly, he didn't get paid for this work until three years later, after a court hearing. Because of this, Martin was unable to continue running the yard, but it was rented out again. In 2002, the last major rebuild at the yard was the 86ft wooden motor yacht *Ginger Dot*.

The Whisstocks site was never a 'redundant boatyard' and many people would have liked to have run a yard here. But it became worth more as a building site than a boat repair shed. The trend had begun to make riverside yards into housing, and the Woodbridge site became very attractive to developers. The Woodbridge district rose up in one voice to fight off this idea and the Whisstocks site changed hands three times. It stood empty for many years, but eventually Suffolk Coastal District Council gave up the fight and granted planning permission for a development including housing. In 2016, twenty-four years after Whisstocks had closed, building began on a new waterside project.

Although both yards had continued building wooden boats for many years, the 'no fibreglass' decision ultimately ended Wood-bridge's life as a boatbuilding centre. Frank Knights told me the story some forty years after it had happened and ended with a smile saying, 'We got it wrong'.

Everson's Boatyard retained its name until 2011 when it became the Woodbridge Boatyard because this was easier to find when searching the internet. Upriver, at Melton, Simon Skeet and Larkman's expanded their boat repair and storage yards. Melton is also the base for Tam Grundy, a marine contractor who maintains moorings and quays and also does dredging and towage with the tugs *Ben Michael* and *Fury*. His lighter was a lifeboat on the North Sea Ferry European Gateway

**Everson's Boatyard in 2015. Photograph: Nick Rowland.**

that capsized off Felixstowe. In 2017 Tam was having a steel mooring lighter *Patricia G*, built, designed by Ben Grundy and welded at Skeet's Melton Boatyard.

Boatbuilding in Woodbridge finished, but it continued at Felixstowe Ferry Boatyard with John White and Andy Moore building wooden fishing boats and this has continued with Andy fitting out new steel and fibreglass hulls for fishing. In 2008, after three years in the building, Andy Moore launched his 46 ton steel multi-cat *Deben Trojan* for maintaining moorings. Over the years, the number of yachts on the River Deben has increased the pressure on space ashore and afloat. The river is organised by mooring committees who are, fortunately, mostly local people. They battle to provide as many moorings as possible without choking up the river.

Woodbridge seems timeless, but nothing stays the same forever, even beside the beautiful Deben. The old era of building new boats at Woodbridge has faded into the background. Yachts and houseboats have taken over the waterside. Behind the waterfront, the narrow streets sprawl happily up the hillside. Tourism fits comfortably into

**Building work on new flats on the Whisstock site. 2017. The *Sae Wylfing* is a half-length replica of the Sutton Hoo ship built for Edwin Gifford to see if the original ship would have sailed.**

the old town, but the new residential Woodbridge has expanded. From the early twentieth century the town has been steadily spreading out and by the twenty-first century, many green fields have become potential building sites. Change has enhanced Woodbridge though and created a lively community and new ventures. In 2017 *The King's River* opera was created for the opening of the Whisstocks development and the documentary film *Life on the Deben* proved hugely popular. Whatever the future holds for the town and its river, there will always be a fascination and value for its long and varied history.